Mel Bay's PRIVATE LES

Modern Blues

Advanced Blues Reharmonizations & Melodic Ideas For Guitar

taught by... Bruce Saunders

ONLINE AUDIO

Track	Content	Track	Content	Track	Content
1	Tuning note	29	Ex. 23 (pg. 26)	55	Ex. 30 (pg. 43)
2	Ex. 1 (pg. 6)	30	Ex. 25 (pg. 28)	56	Ex. 31 (pg. 44)
3	Ex. 2 (pg. 7)	31	Ex. 26 (pg. 29)	57	Ex. 32 (pg. 45)
4	Ex. 3 (pg. 8)	32	Study #6 (pg. 30-31)	58	Ex. 33 (pg. 46)
5	Ex. 4 (pg. 9)	33	Study #7 (pg. 32)	59	Ex. 34 (pg. 47)
6	Ex. 5 (pg. 9)	34	Study #8 (pg. 34-35)	60	Ex. 35 (pg. 47)
7	Ex. 6 (pg. 9)	35	Study #9 (pg. 38)		
8	Ex. 7 (pg. 10)		PRACTICE TRACKS-APPENDIX A		
9	Ex. 8 (pg. 10)	36	F blues slow (pg. 39)		
10	Ex. 9 (pg. 10)	37	F blues fast (pg. 39)		
11	Ex. 10 (pg. 11)	38	B♭ blues slow (pg. 39)		
12	Ex. 11 (pg. 12)	39	B♭ blues fast (pg. 39)		
13	Ex. 12 (pg. 13)	40	G blues slow (pg. 39)		
14	Ex. 13 (pg. 14)	41	G blues fast (pg. 39)		
15	Ex. 14 (pg. 14)	42	D♭ blues slow (pg. 40)		
16	Study #1 (pg. 15)	43	D♭ blues fast (pg. 40)		
17	Study #2 (pg. 16)	44	C minor blues slow (pg. 40)		
18	Ex. 15 (pg. 17)	45	C minor blues fast (pg. 40)		
19	Ex. 16 (pg. 17)	46	C minor 5/4 slow (pg. 40)		
20	Ex. 17 (pg. 18)	47	C minor 5/4 fast (pg. 40)		
21	Ex. 18 (pg. 18)	48	F Parker blues slow (pg. 41)		
22	Ex. 19 (pg. 18)	49	F Parker blues fast (pg. 41)		
23	Study #3 (pg. 19)	50	F Coltrane blues slow (pg. 41)		
24	Ex. 20 (pg. 20)	51	F Coltrane blues fast (pg. 41)		
25	Study #4 (pg. 21)	52	B♭ Coltrane blues slow (pg. 41)		
26	Ex. 21 (pg. 22)	53	B♭ Coltrane blues slow (pg. 41)		
27	Study #5 (pg. 24)		APPENDIX B		
28	Ex. 22 (pg. 25)	54	Ex. 29 (pg. 42)		

To Access the Online Audio Go To:
www.melbay.com/20415BCDEB

Visit us on the Web at www.melbay.com — E-mail us at email@melbay.com

SOME other blues

This book contains a few melodic and harmonic ideas that a guitarist could use when playing a blues. What we will be studying is primarily a twelve-bar, jazz-based blues style but I feel that it is important to listen closely to all blues styles (indeed, to all styles of music). Buy CD's, listen carefully and try to figure out what some other musicians are doing with the blues. There are many, many wonderful musicians, past and present, and part of the excitement of music is discovering a great player that you haven't heard or studied before. It's hard to consider playing the guitar as work but it does take some dedicated practice time to make some of the concepts in this lesson an unconscious part of improvisation. Thanks for checking out this book and I hope you enjoy working with some of the ideas it contains.

chapter one: simple harmonic ideas 4-10

chapter two: fourths 11-25

chapter three: minor blues 26-32

chapter four: more complex harmonic ideas 33-38

appendix a: practice tracks 39-41

appendix b: alternate vertical elements 42-47

chapter one: simple harmonic ideas

Form: Major 12-bar blues

The following is what is considered a standard 12-bar blues in the key of F. This could be considered the skeleton or framework of the blues. Just remember that there are many, many variations but very often the *basic form remains the same.*

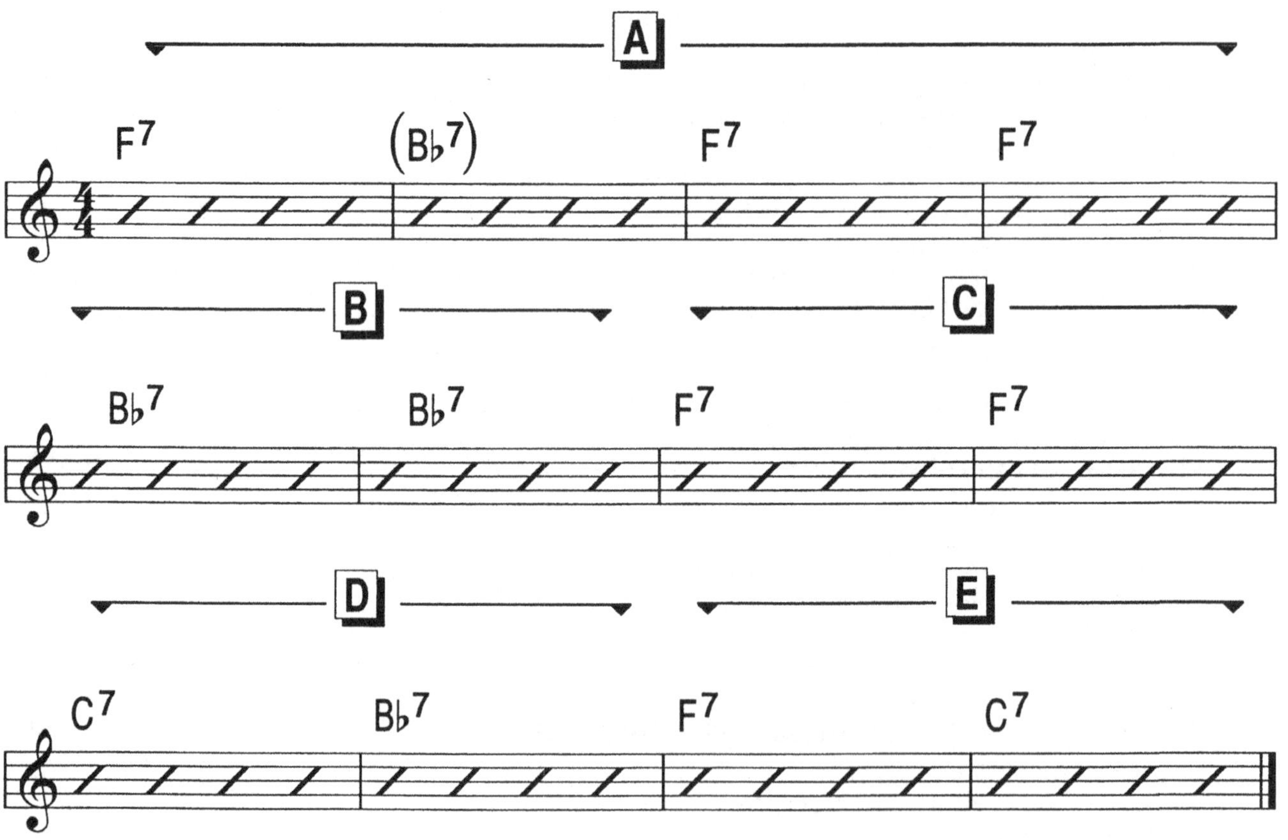

A = The root or the I chord section

B = The IV chord

C = Back to I

D = Important ii-V

E = The turnaround

We're going to explore some different harmonic and melodic possibilities when moving to and from these different sections. I'm starting with the key of F because it's fairly user-friendly on the guitar, there is a long history of blues tunes written in F in the jazz lexicon and mostly because I like the key of F.

basic harmonic elaboration

If you examine the chords below, notice that the skeleton or basic structure of the blues is inside the staff. Above the staff we find a slight elaboration on the basic chord changes. Notice the IV chord in bar two. A closer look shows a secondary dominant function to the chords with alterations. For instance, look at the F7♭9 in bar 4 moving to a B♭7 in bar 5. There are some places in the form where a stronger dominant sound is often used. By a stronger sound I mean chords or scales with more alterations. Bars 4, 8 & 10 are good places to use stronger harmonic language.

Jazz musicians such as Charlie Parker, Wes Montgomery, John Coltrane, Thelonious Monk, Wayne Shorter, Joe Henderson and many others used their own harmonic elaborations to move through a 12-bar blues. We will be exploring just a few of these elaborations in later chapters. For now it's important to memorize the basic structure. I cannot emphasize too strongly the importance of memorization. One common problem I encounter with guitar students is their not knowing *any* tunes from memory. Furthermore, many of these students are incapable of playing a blues form with the same number of bars two choruses in succession, their avowals to the mastery of the blues notwithstanding. Memorize the changes first and then elaborate (musically) on them. This is not an easy thing for many of us to accomplish. Practice is necessary. It's a good thing to memorize melodies as well. There are many, many wonderful blues melodies penned by the great musicians mentioned in the first sentence of this paragraph.

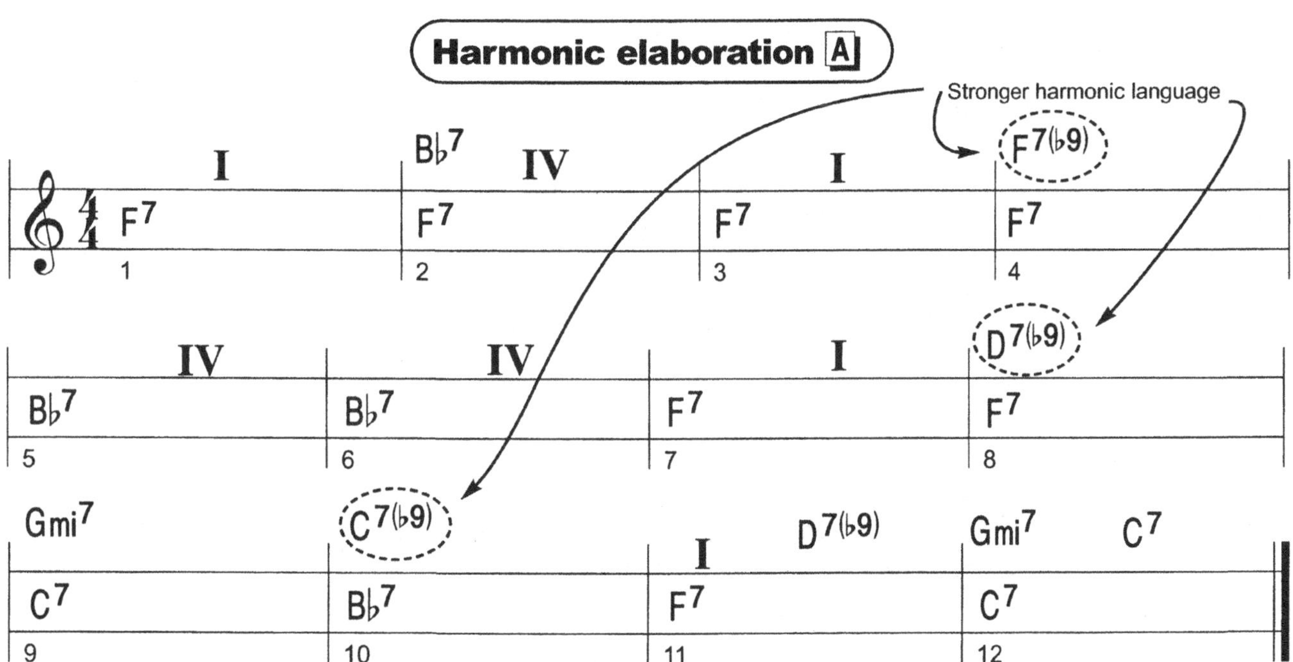

We are going to start with some harmonic and melodic ideas over the blues progression on the preceding page. The first few exercises focus primarily on the use of arpeggios. But rather than utilize an F7 arpeggio over the F7 chord, we'll use what could be considered a Cmi9 or E♭Maj7 arpeggio. A Fmi9 or A♭Maj7 arpeggio works well over the B♭7. This sound is reminiscent of Wes Montgomery or Pat Martino. It's a fairly friendly, non-threatening sound. On the altered dominant chords, an arpeggio borrowed from a melodic minor scale adds some tension. For altered dominant chords, the appropriate melodic minor scale is 1/2 step above the root of the chord. E.g., F7alt. would use the F♯ melodic minor scale. The F♯mi(maj7) arpeggio in bar 4 is borrowed from the F♯ melodic minor scale.

Ex. 1 Arpeggios **# 2 - also use practice tracks 36 & 37**

F7 B♭7 F7 F7alt

♩= 72

Cmi9 or E♭maj9 arp.

A♭maj9 or Fmi9 arp.

F♯mi(Maj7) arpeggio

B♭7 B♭7 F7 D7alt

E♭mi(Maj7) arpeggio

This is a continuation of the arpeggio idea from the previous page. This time the blues is in the key of B♭ but the arpeggio ideas are based on the same respective harmonies. For B♭7, the arpeggio used is Fmi9 or A♭maj9. For E♭7 the arpeggios are based on B♭mi9 (or D♭maj9). One way to put this into a kind of musical shorthand is to think "for the Wes sound I think I'll play a major 7/9 arpeggio down a whole step from the root (tune's over)." Or, for the Martino vibe, think min7 up a fifth. So, F7 = E♭Maj7/9 or Cmi7. Now, practice this over lots of blues choruses in lots of keys.

Ex. 2 B♭ blues arpeggios **# 3 - also use practice tracks 38 & 39**

Here's some more of the same. However, this time I tried to keep the same arpeggio through more than one chord change. For instance, a Cmi9 arpeggio on both F7 and B♭7. This has a sound reminiscent of the beginning of John Coltrane's solo on "Cousin Mary" **[<u>John Coltrane</u> *Giant Steps* (Atlantic 1311-2 rec. 1959)].**

Ex. 3 Arpeggios **# 4 - also use practice tracks 36 & 37**

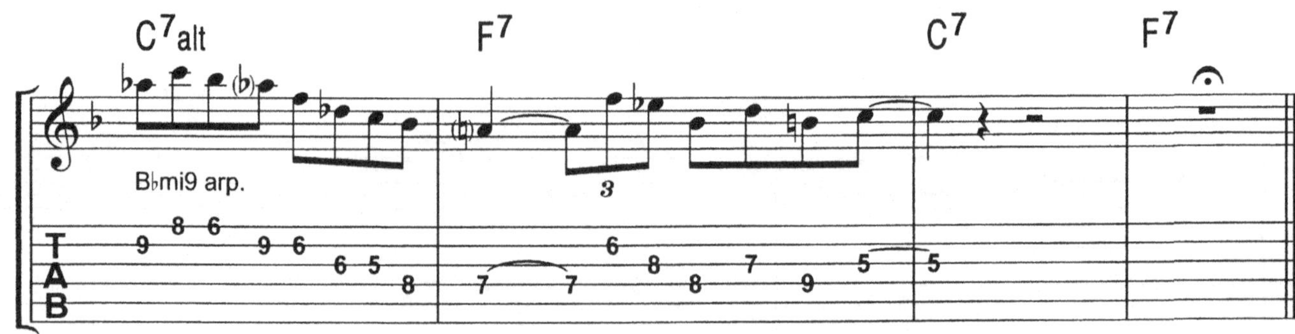

In the following exercises I have taken pairs of chords that you could consider the I and the IV chords in a major blues. Over these pairs I have written some arpeggio scenarios that you might want to use to further develop your own ideas. This has a vague resemblance to a motivic sound that Coltrane used a lot and that we will be exploring further in the lesson.

Ex. 4 G blues - motivic arpeggios **# 5 - also use practice tracks 40 & 41**

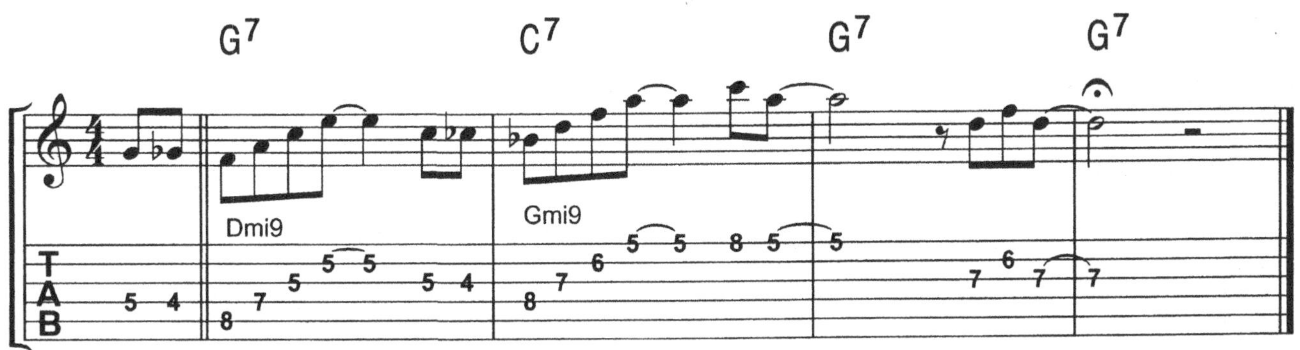

Ex. 5 Motivic arpeggios **# 6**

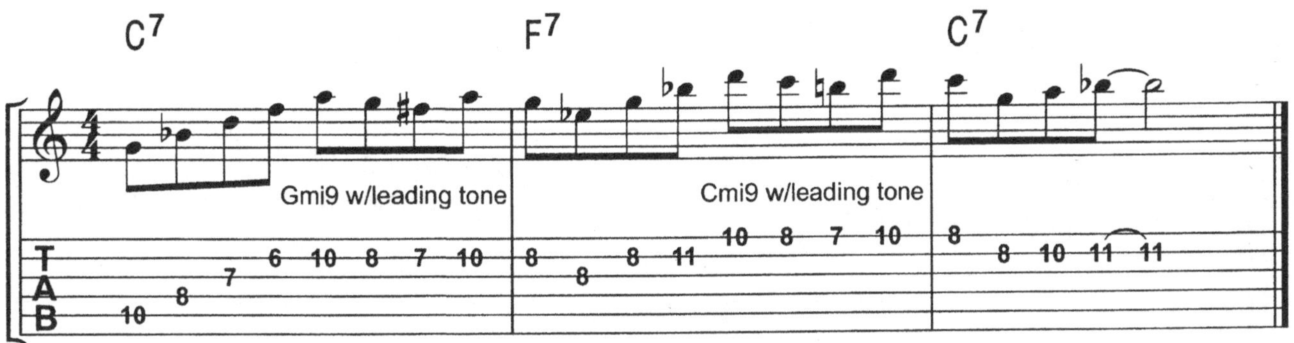

Ex. 6 Motivic arpeggios **# 7 - also use practice tracks 40 & 41**

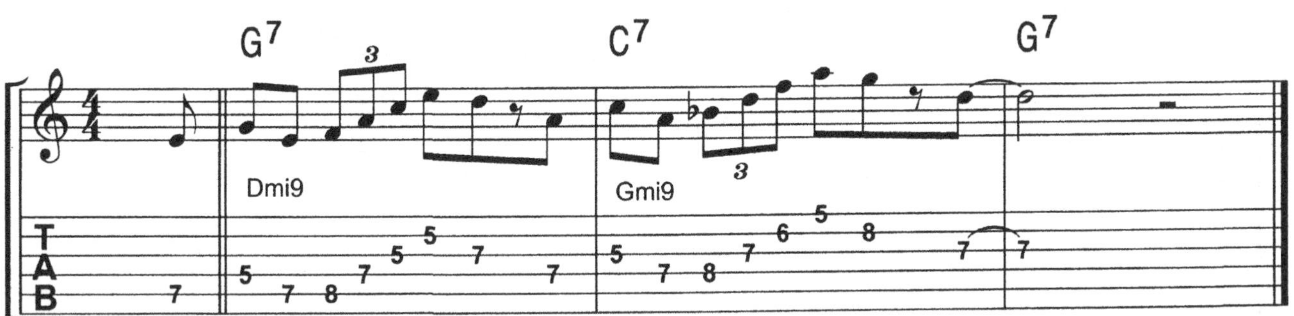

Ex. 7 D♭ blues - motivic arpeggios **# 8 - also use practice tracks 42 & 43**

Ex. 8 Motivic arpeggio ideas **# 9 - also use practice tracks 36 & 37**

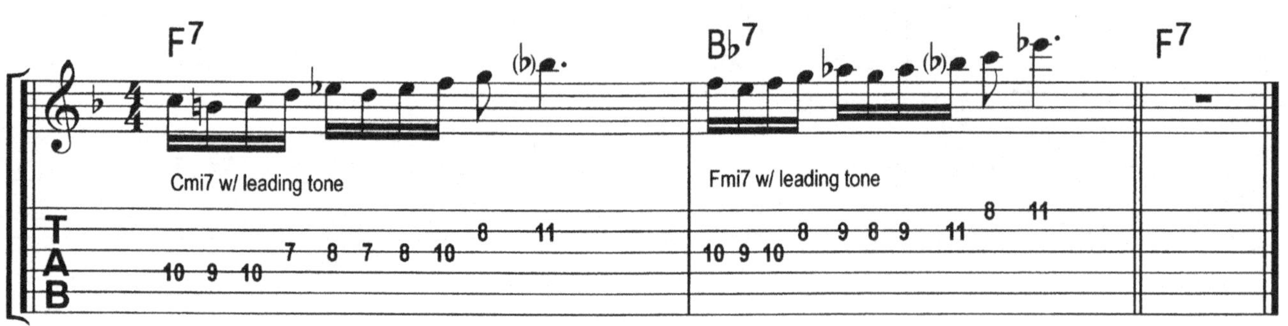

Ex. 9 Motivic arpeggios **# 10 - also use practice tracks 38 & 39**

chapter two: fourths

One technique that gives a modern sound to a blues is the use of fourths. Blues heads such as "In 'n Out" (Joe Henderson *In 'n Out* (**Blue Note CDP 724382915621 Rec. 1964**), "Blues On The Corner" (McCoy Tyner *The Real McCoy (***Blue Note CDP 7465122 Rec. 1967**) and numerous others by such jazz artists as Wayne Shorter, Miles Davis and Woody Shaw make extensive use of fourths. Fourths give an open sound to comping or to solos. With this in mind, what follows are some fourth voicings that can be used for a blues in the key of F. I'll show you how they might be used for comping or soloing over a 12-bar blues.

F7 FOURTH VOICINGS
Harmonize a F Mixolydian Scale in fourths
F Mixolydian = Fifth mode of B♭ Major Scale

Ex. 10

F7 - comping fourth voicings

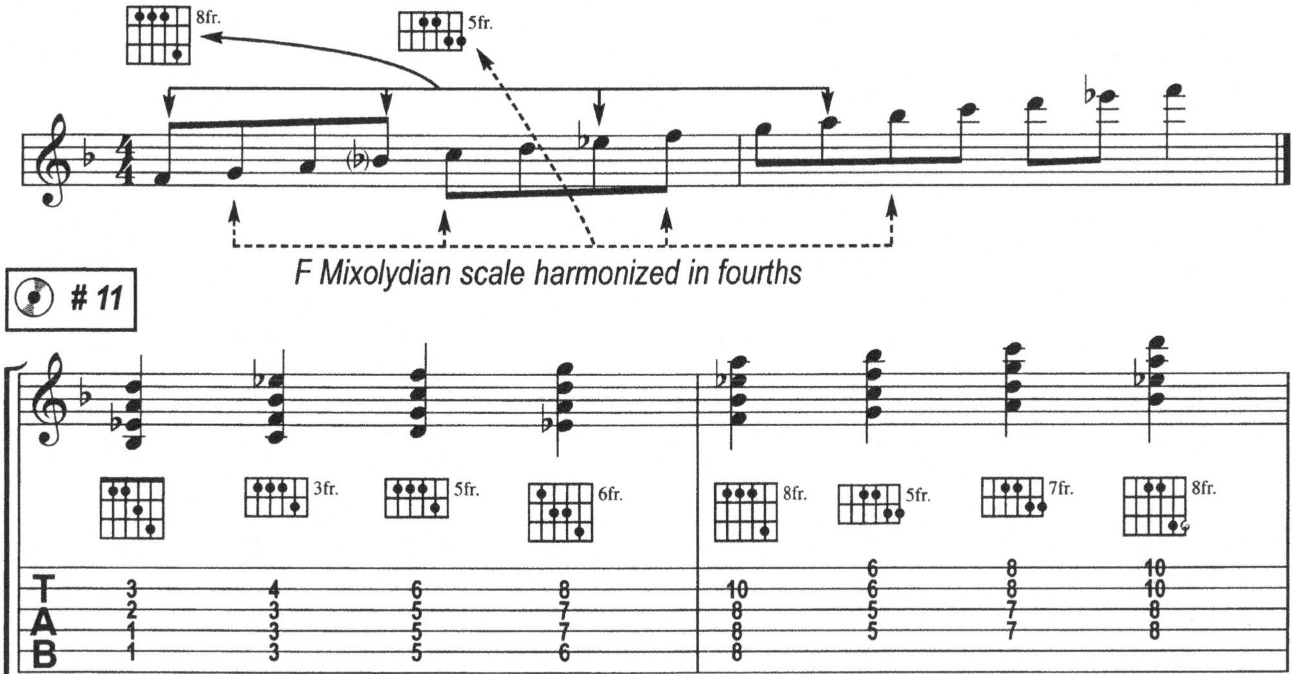

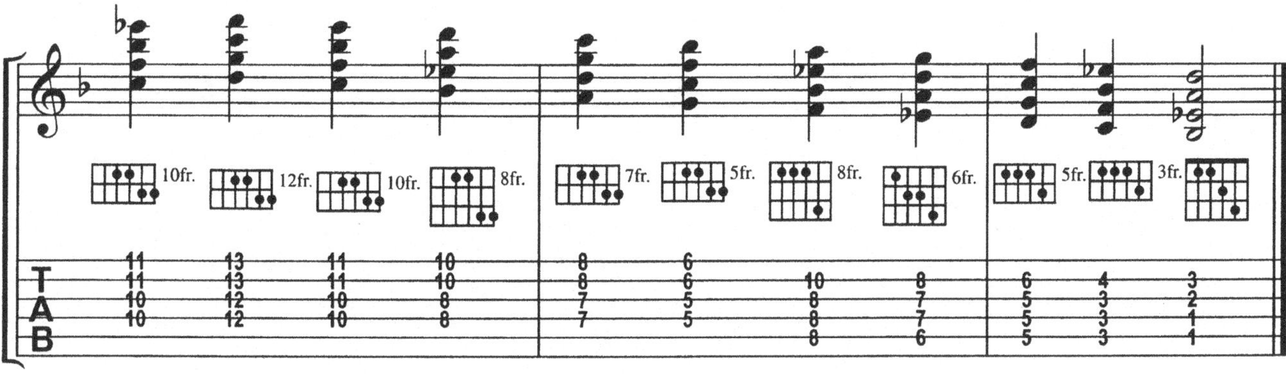

B♭7 FOURTH VOICINGS
Harmonize a B♭ Mixolydian Scale in fourths
B♭ Mixolydian = Fifth mode of E♭ Major Scale

Ex. 11 B♭7 - comping fourth voicings **# 12 - also use practice tracks 38 & 39**

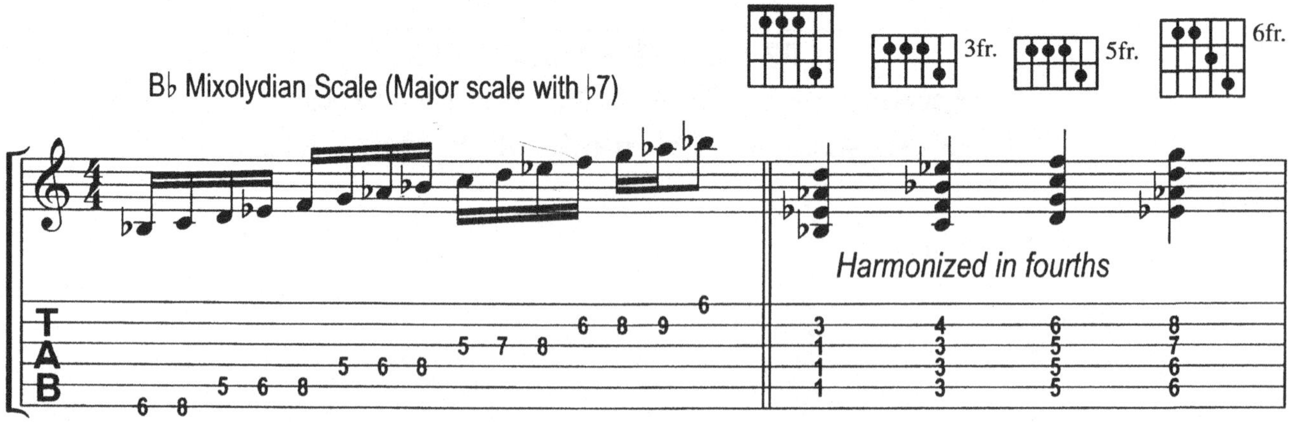

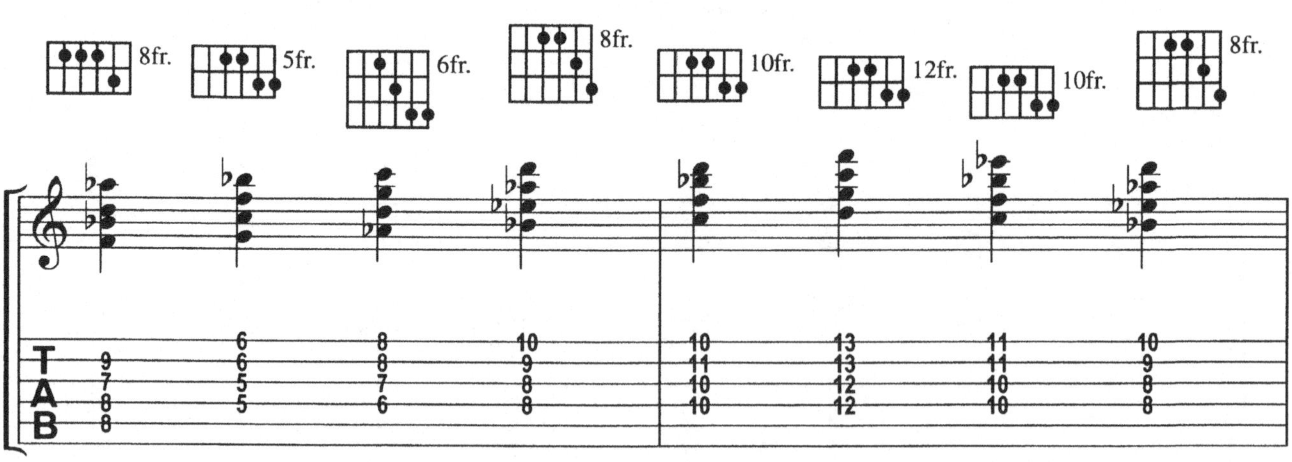

B♭ Mixolydian Scale (Major scale with ♭7)
3fr.
5fr.
6fr.
Harmonized in fourths
T
A
B

8fr.
5fr.
6fr.
8fr.
10fr.
12fr.
10fr.
8fr.
T
A
B

6fr.
5fr.
8fr.
6fr.
5fr.
3fr.
T
A
B

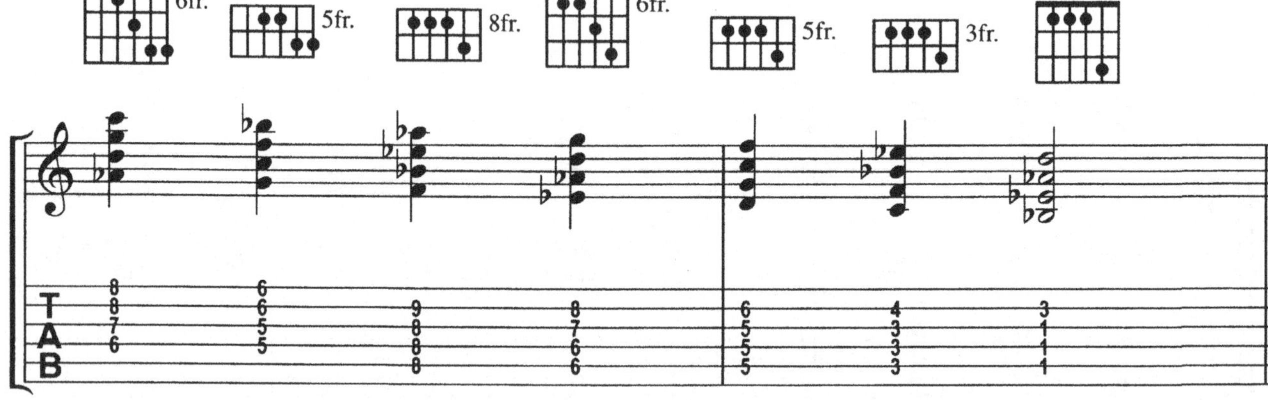

Another technique used by modern jazz players is the use of melodic minor scales and modes. One very common practice is to use a melodic minor 1/2 step above the root of dominant seventh altered chords. For example, C7alt. = D♭ melodic minor, D7 alt. = E♭ melodic minor, etc. These melodic minor scales can be harmonized in fourths just like any other scale or mode. You might also consider this seventh melodic minor mode below to be the **altered scale**.

C7alt. = D♭ Melodic Minor Scale in fourths

Ex. 13

D♭ melodic minor - comping in fourths # 14

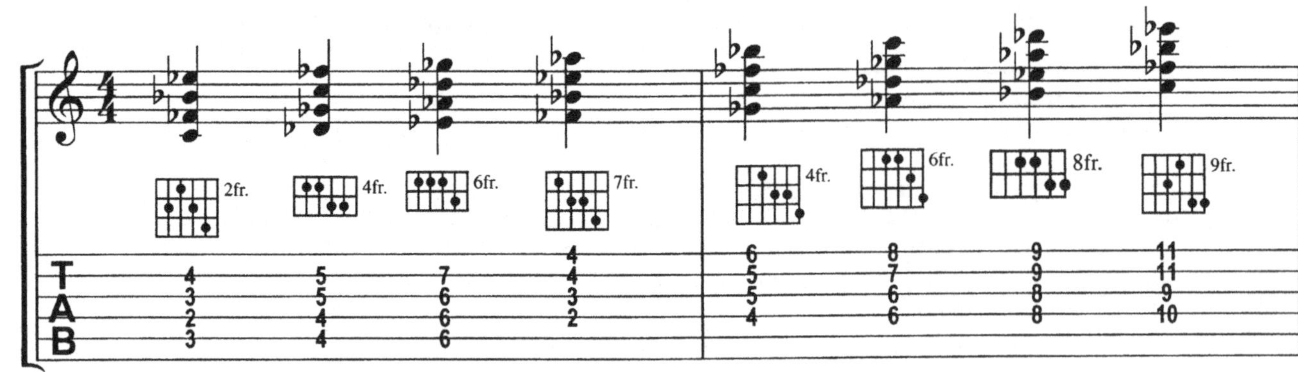

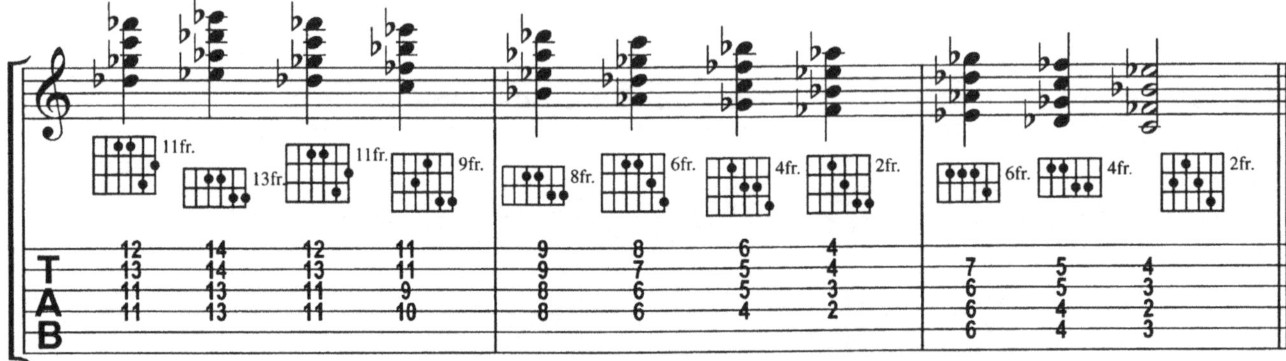

D7alt. = E♭ Melodic Minor Scale in fourths

Ex. 14

E♭ melodic minor - comping in fourths # 15

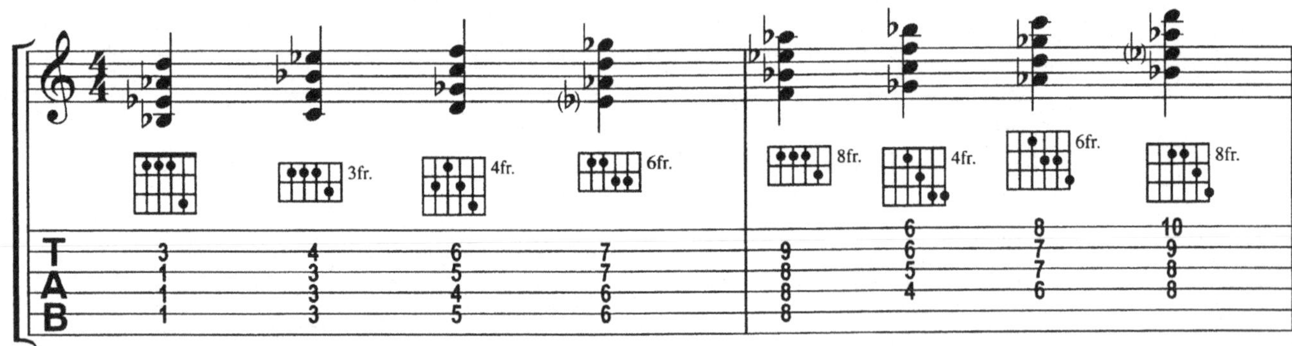

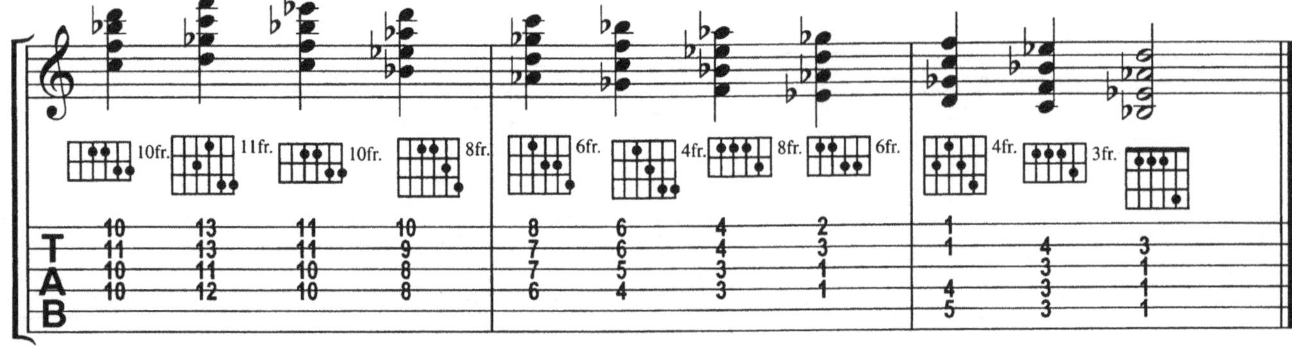

Now, some choruses of the blues in F using some of these fourth voicings.

Study No. 1 Blues in F - comping four-note fourth voicings

 # 16 - also use practice tracks 36 & 37

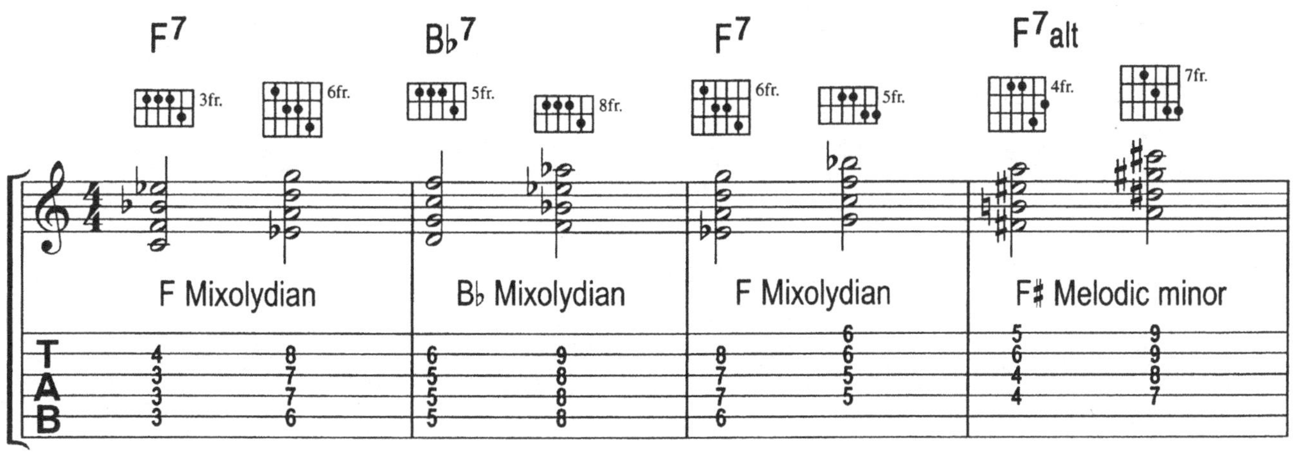

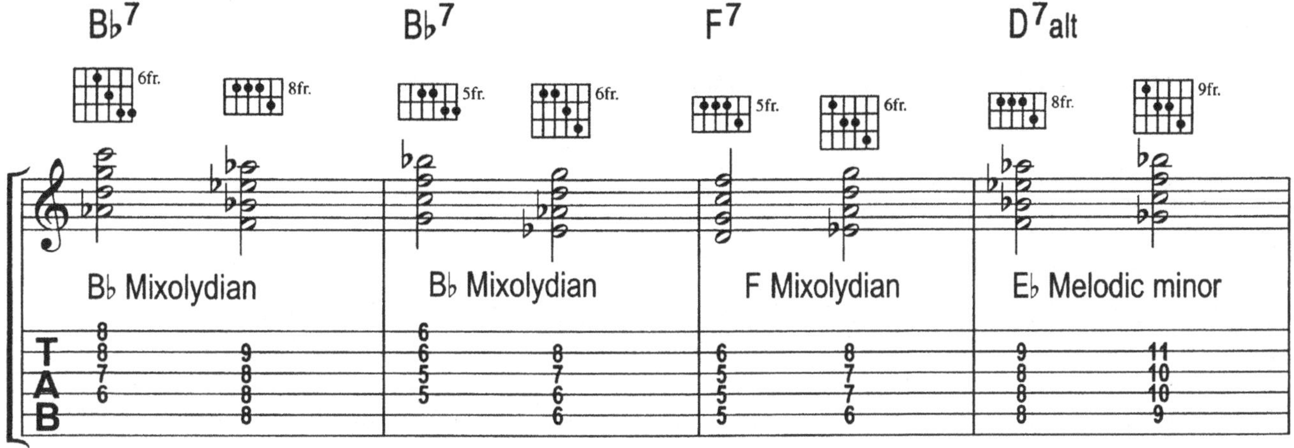

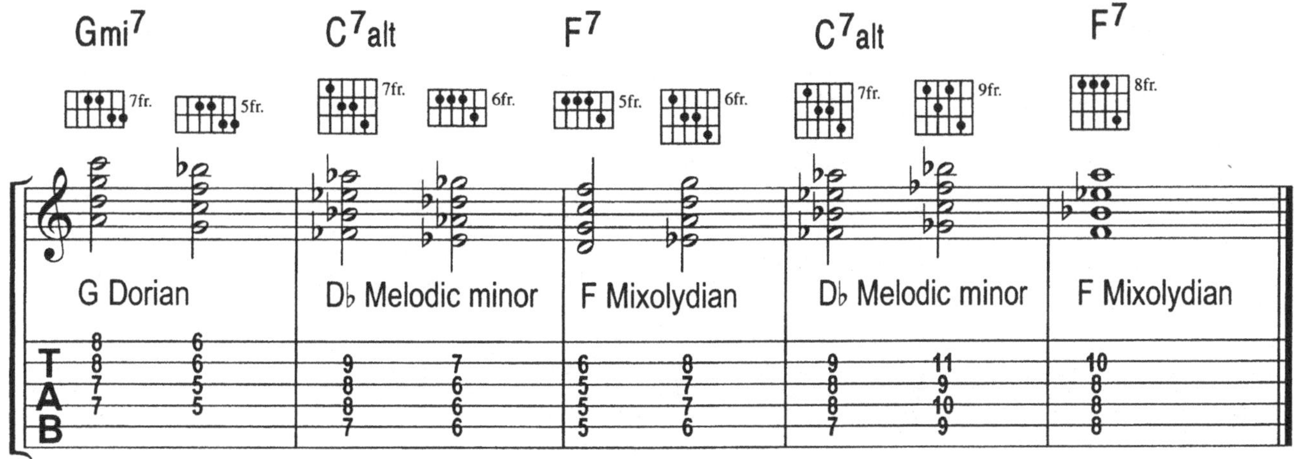

It's got a thing. Some of the voicings have more weight than others. It takes some practice to improvise using these fourth voicings. It's important to remember that no matter what the voicing, the prime directive is a solid, well-considered time feel, regardless of style.

Study No. 2 Blues in F - comping four-note fourth voicings

 # 17 - also use practice tracks 36 & 37

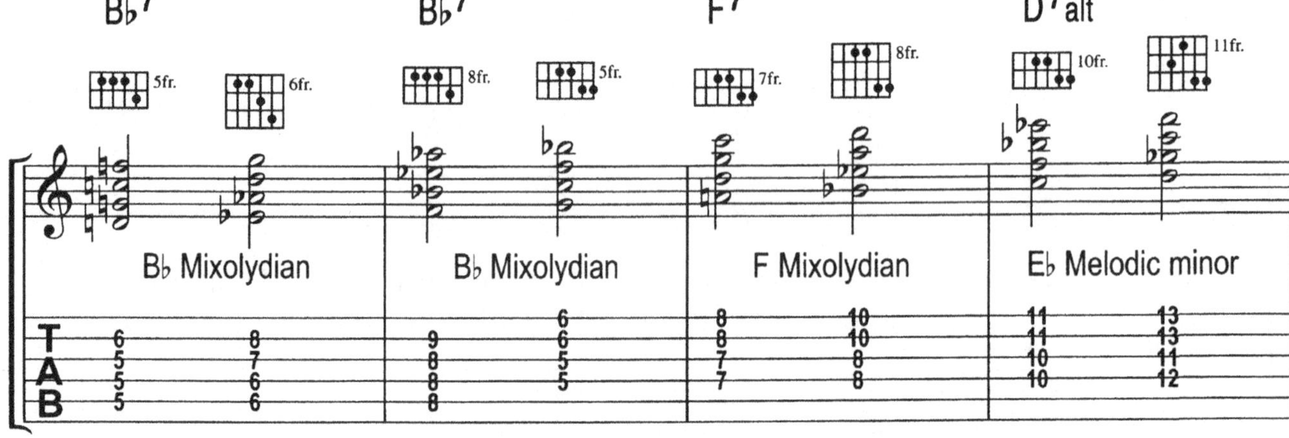

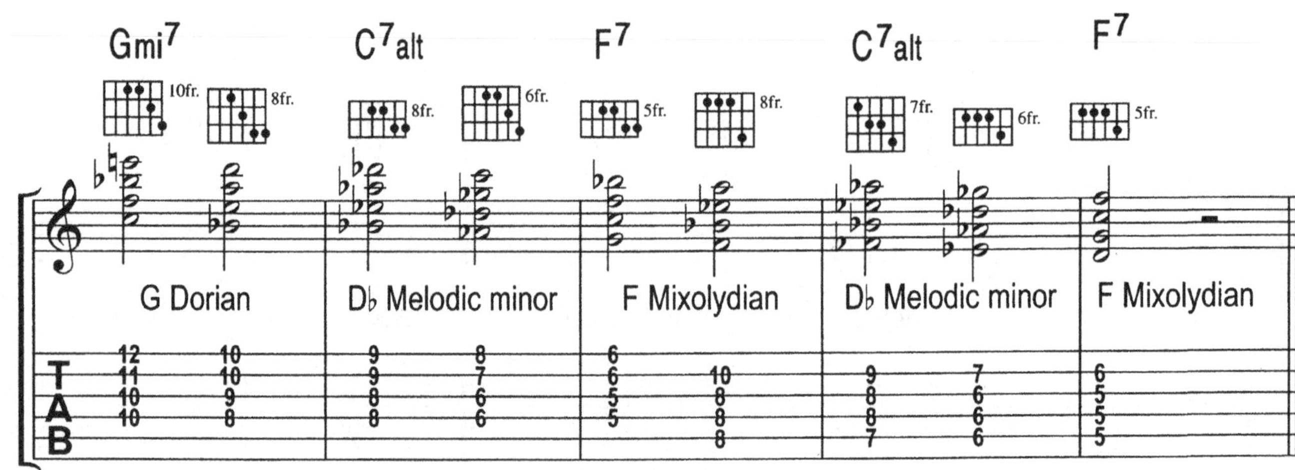

Four voices in fourths can be somewhat unwieldy so one option is to remove a voice, stacking two fourth intervals instead of three.

Stacking three voices in fourths

F Mixolydian scale

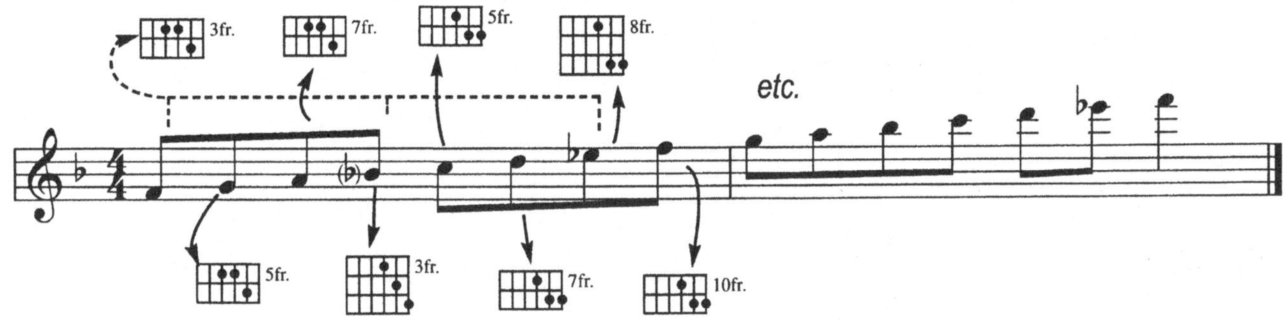

Ex. 15 F Mixolydian - three-voice fourth chords # 18

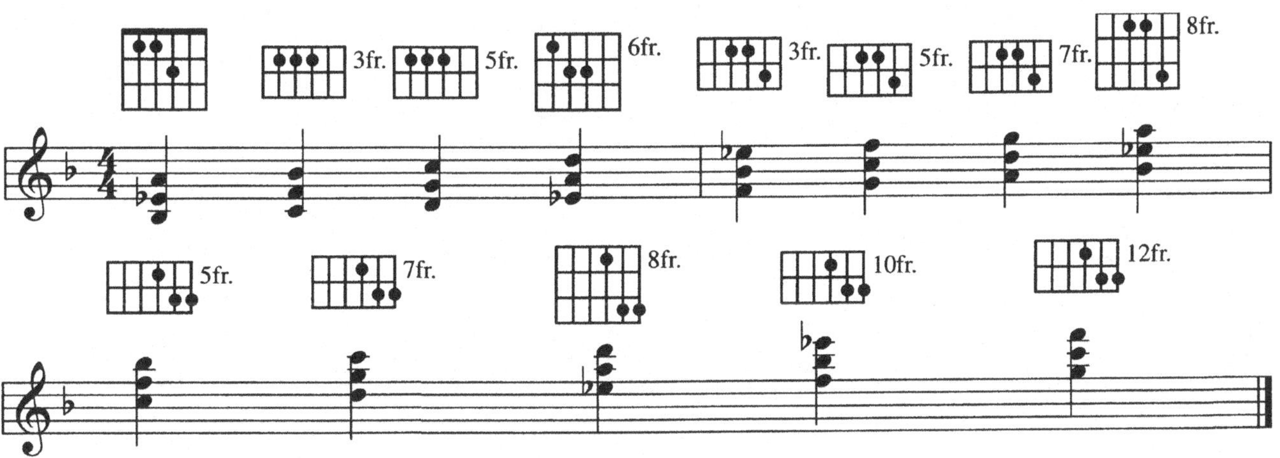

Ex. 16 B♭ Mixolydian - three-voice fourth chords # 19

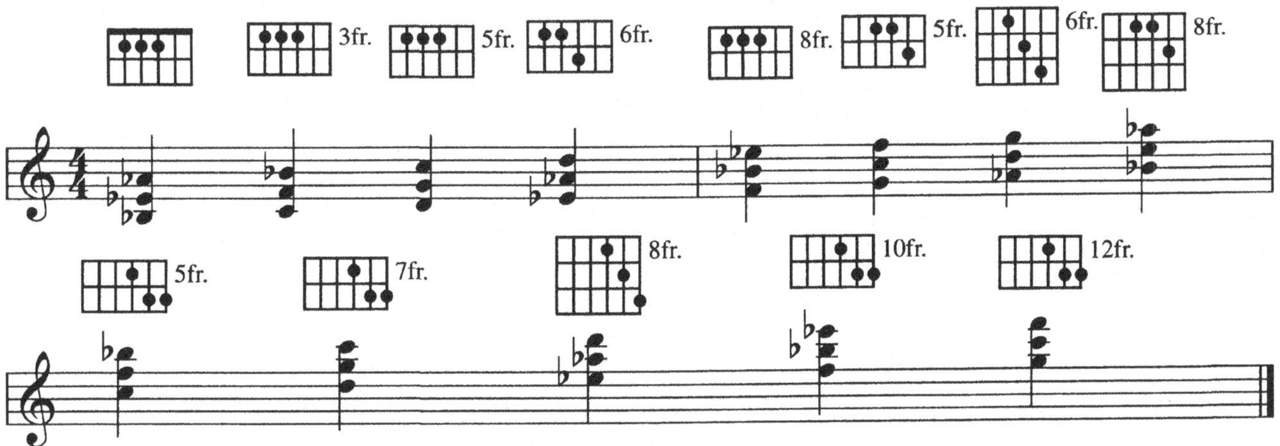

Ex. 17 F♯ Melodic minor - three-voice fourth chords # 20

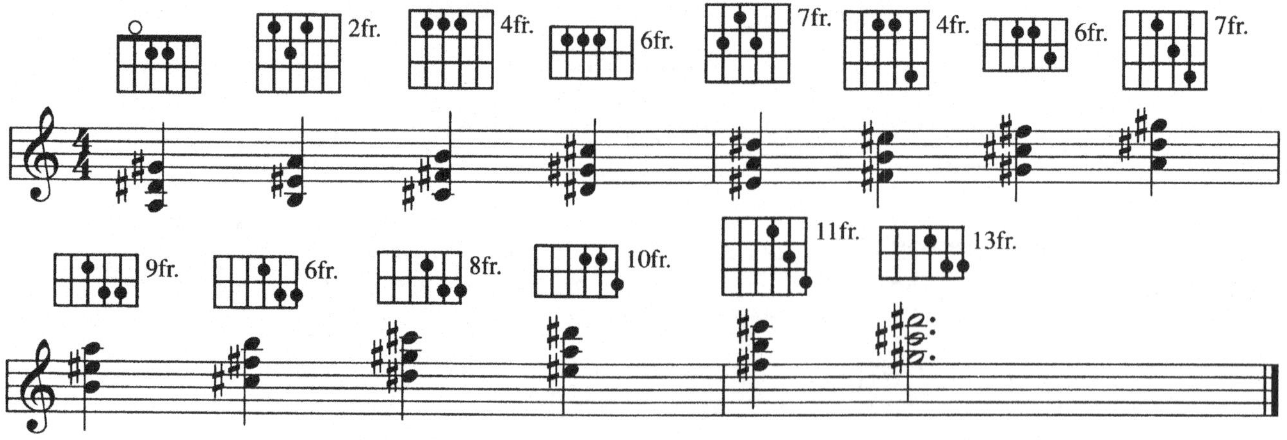

Ex. 18 E♭ Melodic minor - three-voice fourth chords # 21

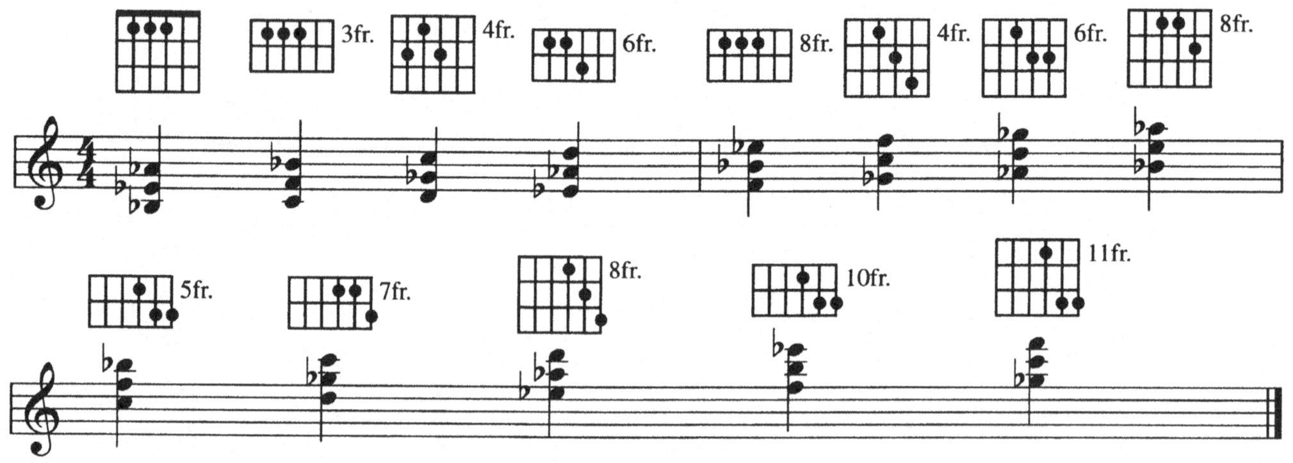

Ex. 19 D♭ Melodic minor - three-voice fourth chords # 21

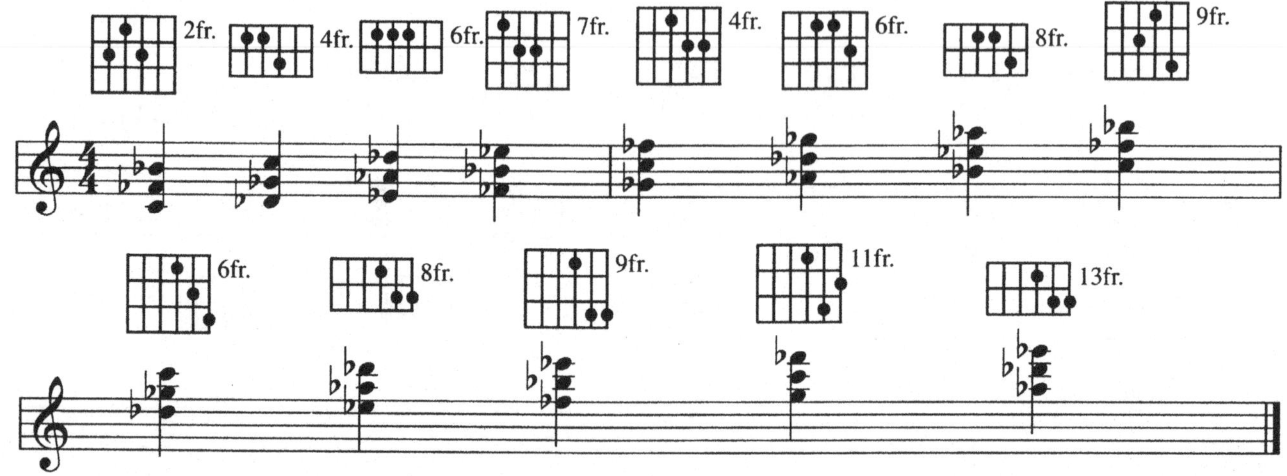

Study No. 3 Blues in F - comping three-note fourth voicings

 # 20 - also use practice tracks 36 & 37

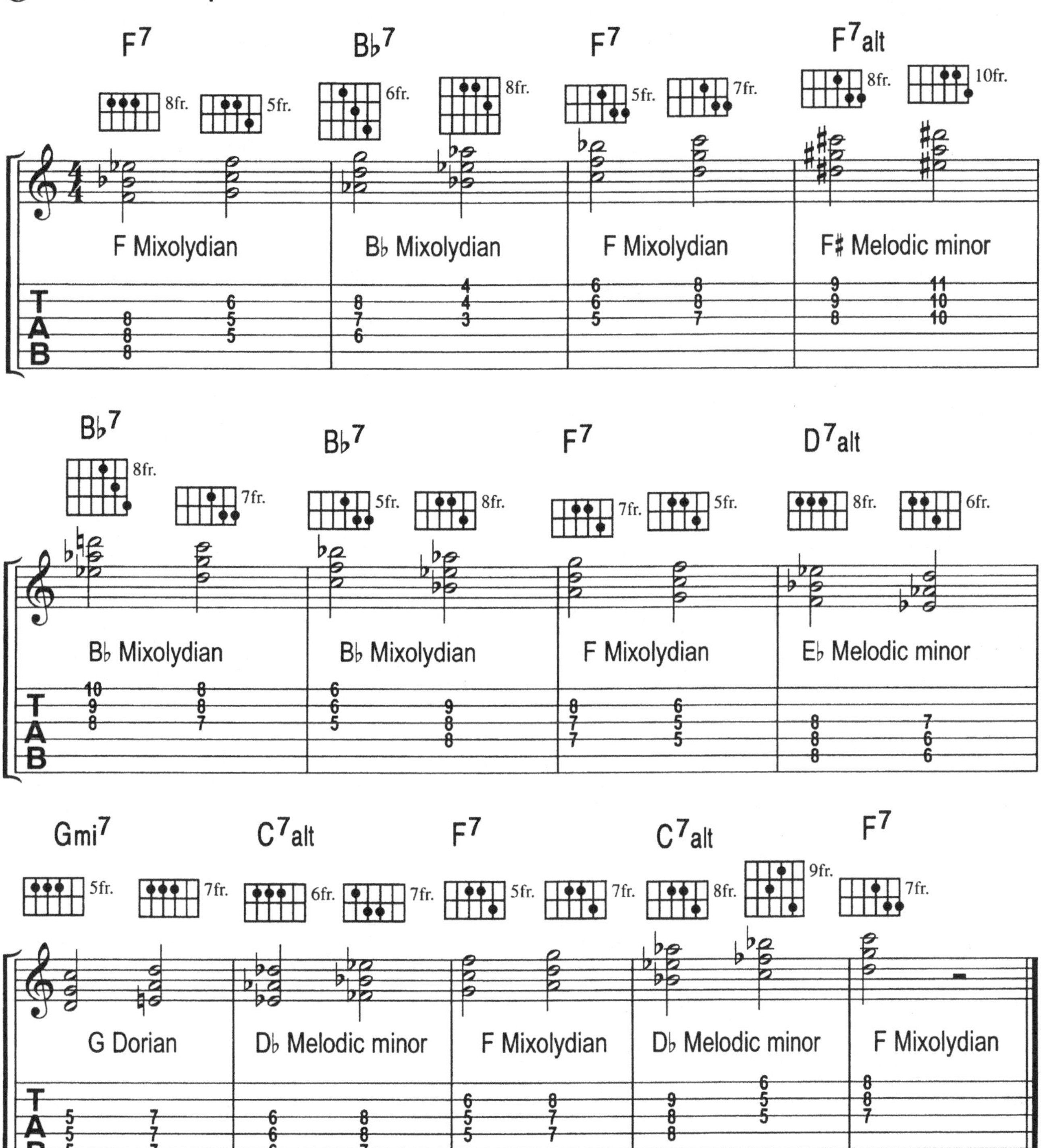

These three-note voicings are easier to break up into single-line ideas than four-note voicings. Playing fourths exclusively throughout a solo or even for a chorus is akin to painting with only one color. Great blues solos are balanced rhythmically, harmonically and melodically. For most musicians it takes some sincere practice time to add a technique such as the use of fourths to the palette of improvisational colors. In Exercise # 20, I have taken Study # 3 and arpeggiated the voicings.

Ex. 20 F blues - arpeggiated three-note fourth voicings **# 24 - also use practice tracks 36 & 37**

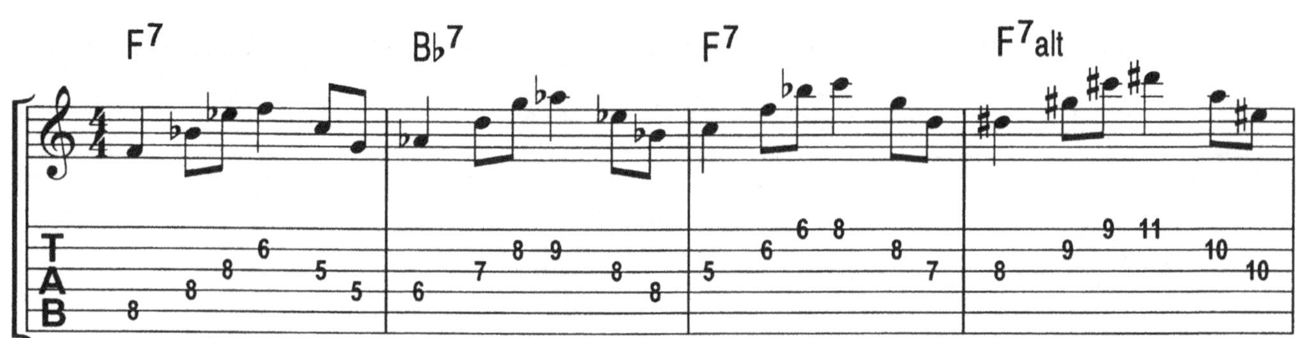

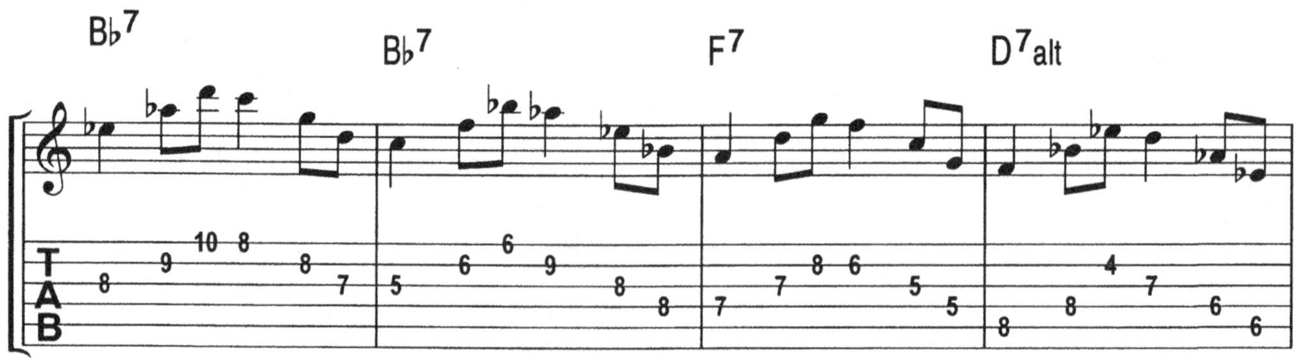

Study No. 4

Blues in F - comping three-note fourth voicings **# 25 - also use practice tracks 36 & 37**

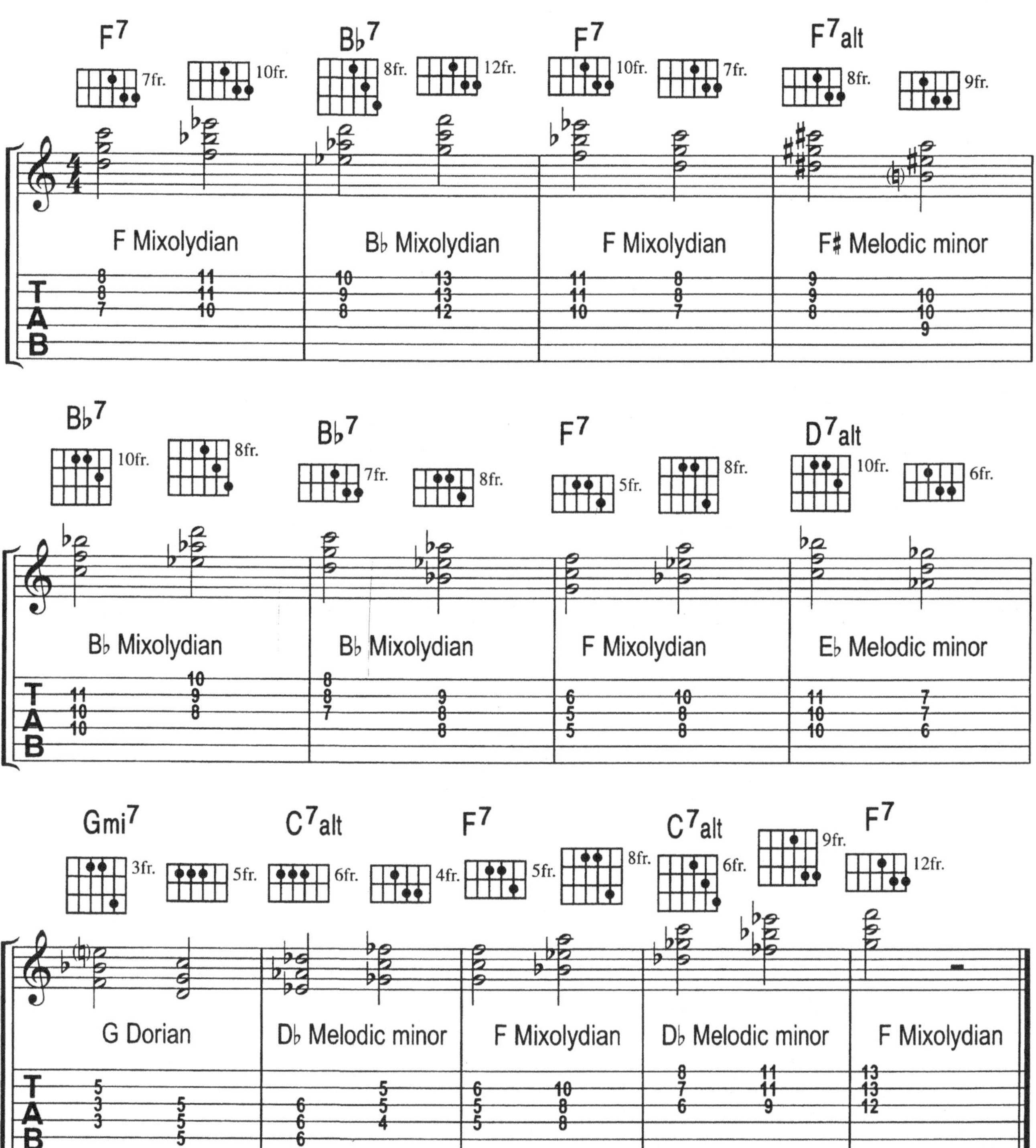

The next example is Study no. 4 played as quarter note triplet arpeggios.

Ex. 21 F blues - arpeggiated three-note fourth voicings **# 26 - also use practice tracks 36 & 37**

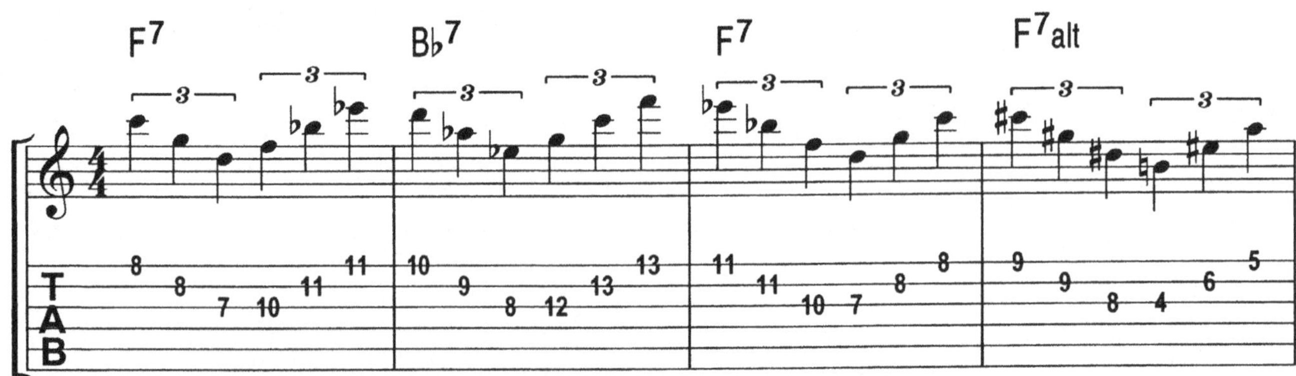

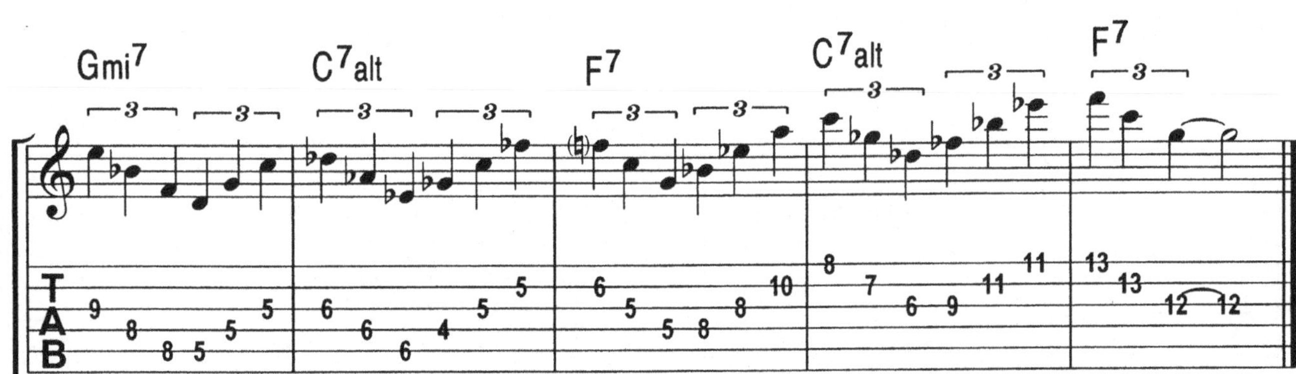

You may have found playing fourths on a standard blues progression in the ways I have suggested a little tricky. This may be partly because musicians who make extensive use of fourths (Joe Henderson and McCoy Tyner, for instance) will often substitute more open chord changes over a 12-bar blues that allow for greater freedom. A blues form that uses only three chords over which to improvise could make these voicings more accessible. The fourth voicings for the E♭maj7♯11 are below. Since F7 is a mode of B♭ major, you could use these voicings for F7 also.

This blues was written with Joe Henderson and McCoy Tyner in mind but is named *Blues for J.T.* in honor of the great guitarist John Thomas. J.T. lives in Boston, recorded with Joe Henderson and plays an intense, swinging, post-bebop style. This melody reminds me of something John might play.

Study No. 5 - Blues for J.T. F blues using fourths # 27

(Use last two bars as intro / outro)

This is a solo an improvisor like Joe Henderson might play on the modified blues changes of *Blues for J.T.* You might notice an angular sound to some of this solo but there is nothing that is too difficult to play with a little practice. Notice the use of fourths combined with stepwise movement. Look for "side-slipping" examples where the improvisor moves 1/2 step away from the original chord or key. At times the notes don't seem to fit the chord above the staff but a great improvisor like Joe Henderson would be indicating an alternate harmonic structure or just playing what he heard at the moment. See if you can figure out what harmonies are indicated by the accidentals (like in measures 6-8).

Ex. 22 Blues for J.T. - one chorus solo # 28

chapter three: minor blues

As a guitarist, you are probably very familiar with pentatonics like the one below.

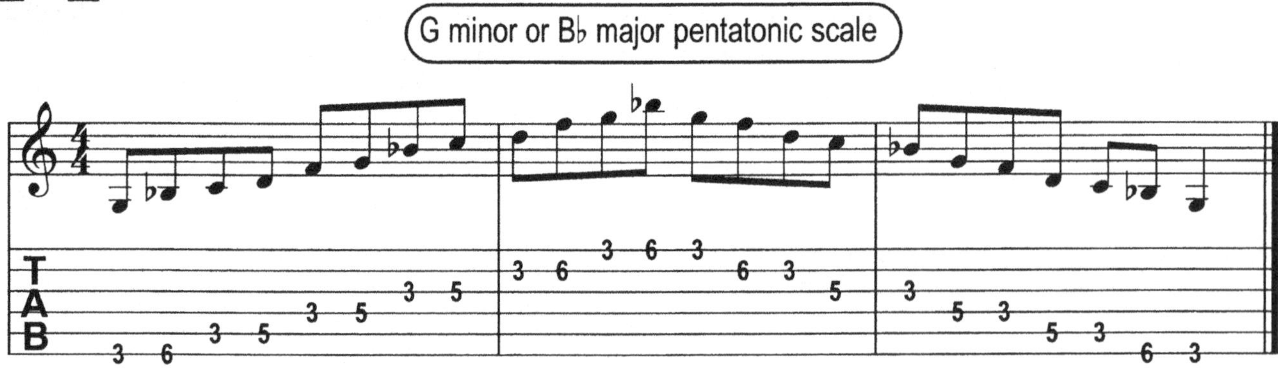

Jazz musicians such as Joe Henderson, McCoy Tyner, John Coltrane, Chick Corea, Michael Brecker and many, many other great musicians used pentatonics in a much different way than the average guitarist. While a typical guitarist might use the scale above to improvise over G7 or B♭7, a saxophonist might use this scale to improvise on E7alt., A♭Maj7♯11 or Cmi7. We're going to explore just one example of a pentatonic scale you probably have played before but we'll be using this five-note scale slightly differently. Listen to the sound of Gmi7 pentatonic in Ex. 23 played over a Cmi7 chord. Notice how the notes in the Gmi7 pentatonic scale relate to the Cmi7 chord. For instance, the root of Gmi7 (the note G) is the fifth of the Cmi7. The ♭3rd in the Gmi7 pentatonic is the ♭7 of Cmi7 and so on.

Ex. 23 Gmi7 Pentatonic over Cmi7 chord # 29

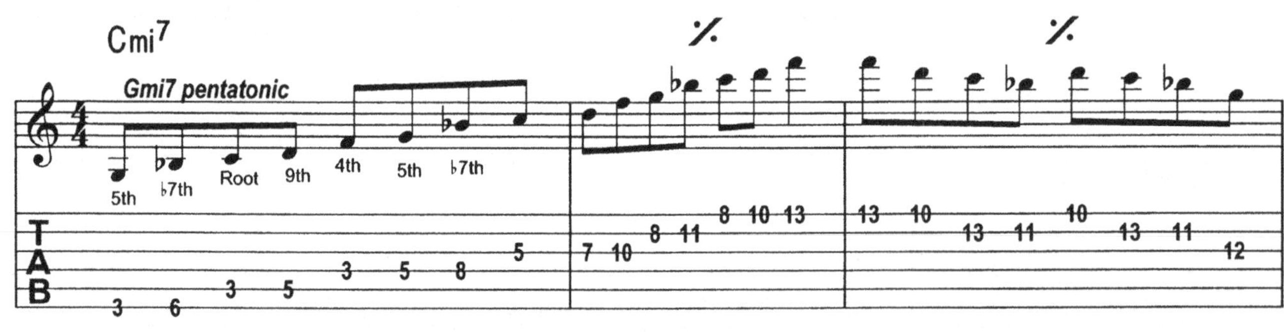

The pentatonic scale is used a perfect 5th up from the root of the mi7 chord. If you like the sound of this, it would be a good thing to memorize this relationship.

mi7 chord	pentatonic scale
Cmi7	Gmi7
Fmi7	Cmi7
Bbmi7	Fmi7
E♭mi7	B♭mi7
A♭mi7	E♭mi7
D♭mi7	A♭mi7
G♭mi7	D♭mi7
Bmi7	F♯mi7
Emi7	Bmi7
Ami7	Emi7
Dmi7	Ami7
Gmi7	Dmi7

Just like the major blues, there are some key areas in a minor blues where the use of stronger harmonic language is appropriate. You might think of these areas as secondary dominant areas.

These secondary dominant areas are not strictly defined. They don't necessarily start on beat 1 of measure 4 or end on beat 1 of measure 5, etc.

Ex. 24

C minor blues **also use practice tracks 44 & 45**

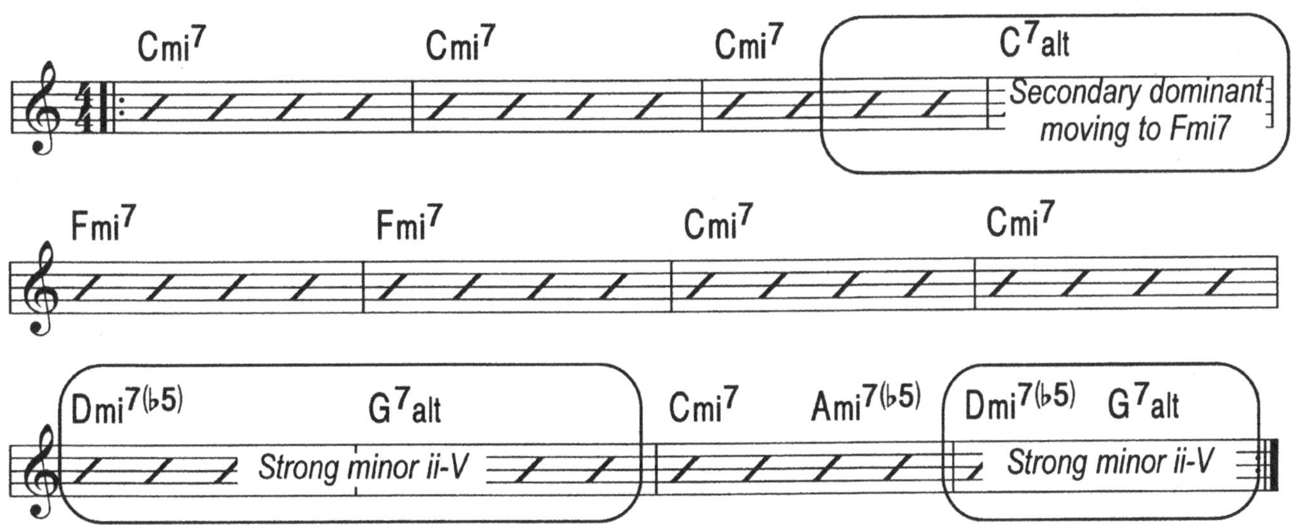

Soon we are going to use pentatonic scales and mix them with some scales and chords that fulfill a dominant function. Concerning dominant functions, let's look at harmonic minor (we'll also be using the melodic minor chords and scales we covered in Chapter 2). Harmonic minor scales work well when the dominant resolves to a minor chord (like in a minor blues). For instance, **G7♭9♭13 = C harmonic minor.**

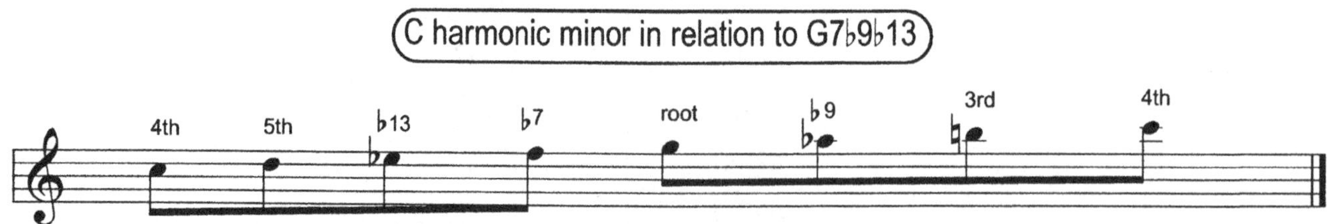

dom7♭9♭13 chord	harmonic minor scale
C7♭9♭13	F harmonic minor
F7♭9♭13	B♭ harmonic minor
B♭7♭9♭13	E♭ harmonic minor
E♭7♭9♭13	A♭ harmonic minor
A♭7♭9♭13	D♭ harmonic minor
D♭7♭9♭13	G♭ harmonic minor
G♭7♭9♭13	B harmonic minor
B7♭9♭13	E harmonic minor
E7♭9♭13	A harmonic minor
A7♭9♭13	D harmonic minor
D7♭9♭13	G harmonic minor
G7♭9♭13	C harmonic minor

You can use this harmonic minor as a linear element and also as a *vertical* element (chords). **Please see Appendix B for some harmonic minor chord voicings with which you can experiment.**

Ex. 25 C harmonic minor as a linear element # 30

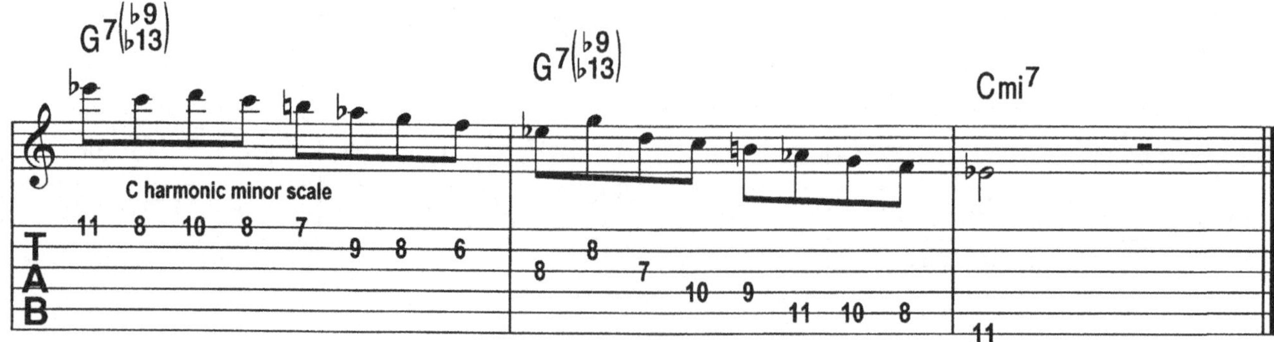

A player from the bebop era such as Charlie Parker or Grant Green might use harmonic minor in a very linear fashion (like in Ex. 25) but the use of wider intervals became more prevalent in the post-bop years. Many post-bop players will mix pentatonic scales, harmonic minor, melodic minor, sideslipping, reharmonization & many other sounds in their solos. The next exercise is intended to open up the sound of a harmonic minor scale.

Ex. 26 C harmonic minor exercise (G7♭9♭13 = C harmonic minor) # 31

G7(♭9 ♯5)

C harmonic minor scale

Study No. 6

C minor blues using pentatonics, melodic & harmonic minor scales

32 - also use practice tracks 44 & 45

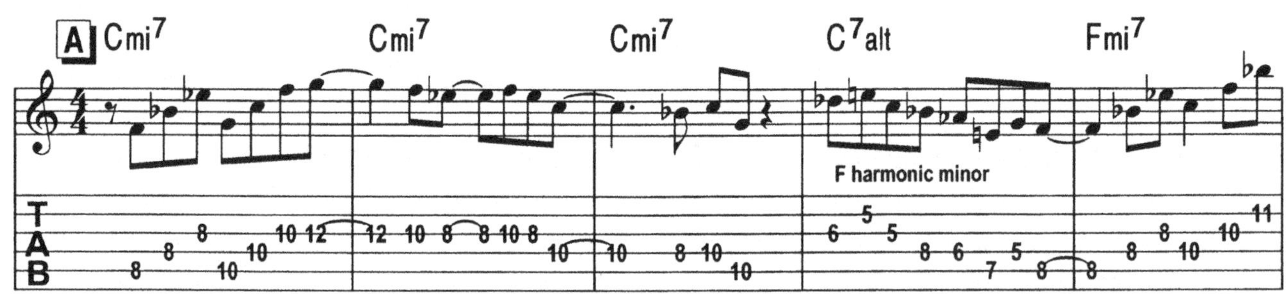

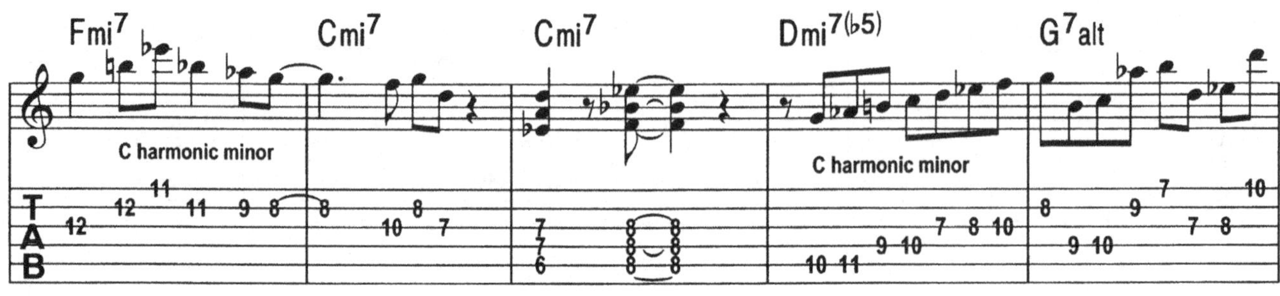

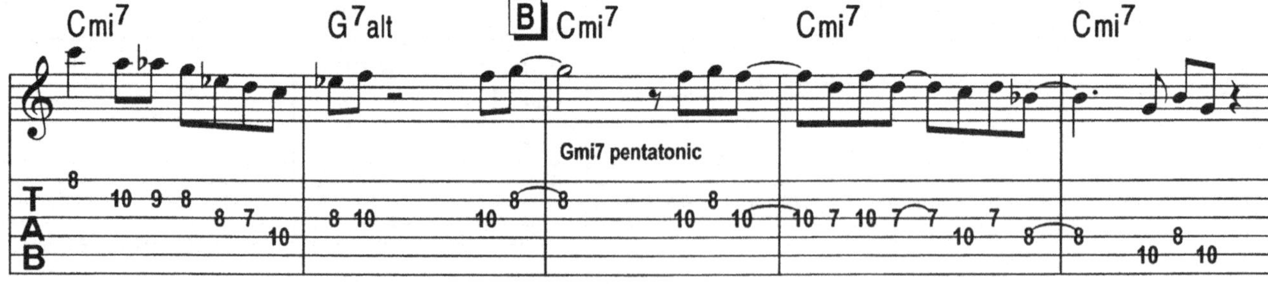

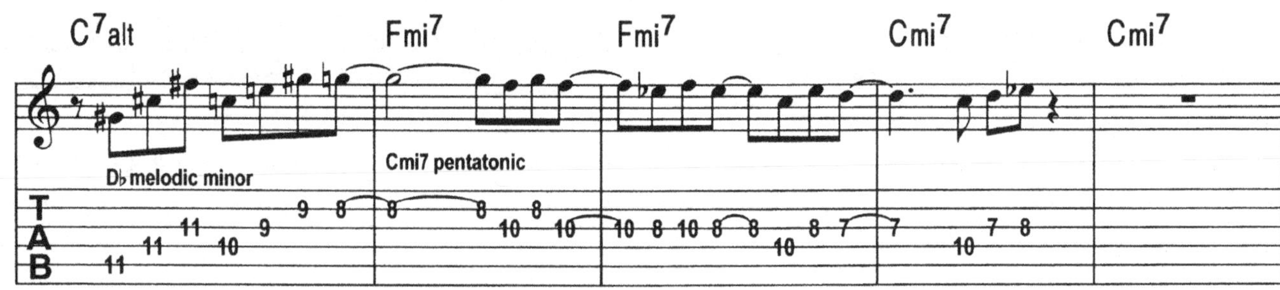

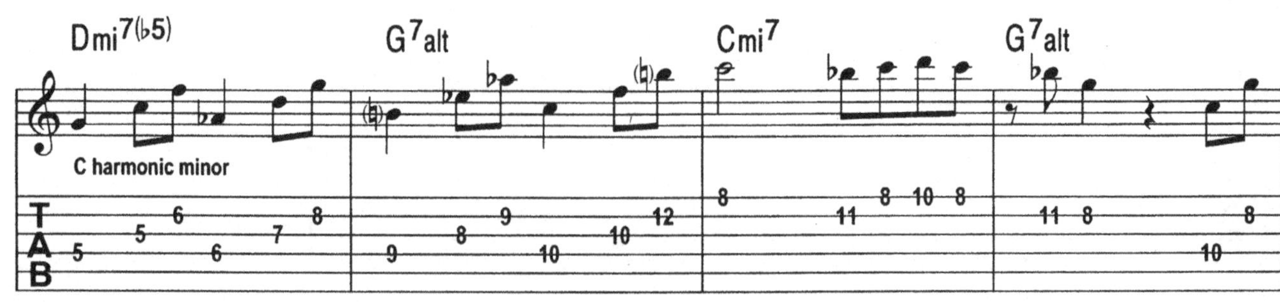

Study No. 6 (continued)

Study No. 7

5/4 C minor blues (groups of three over five) **# 33 - also use practice tracks 46 & 47**

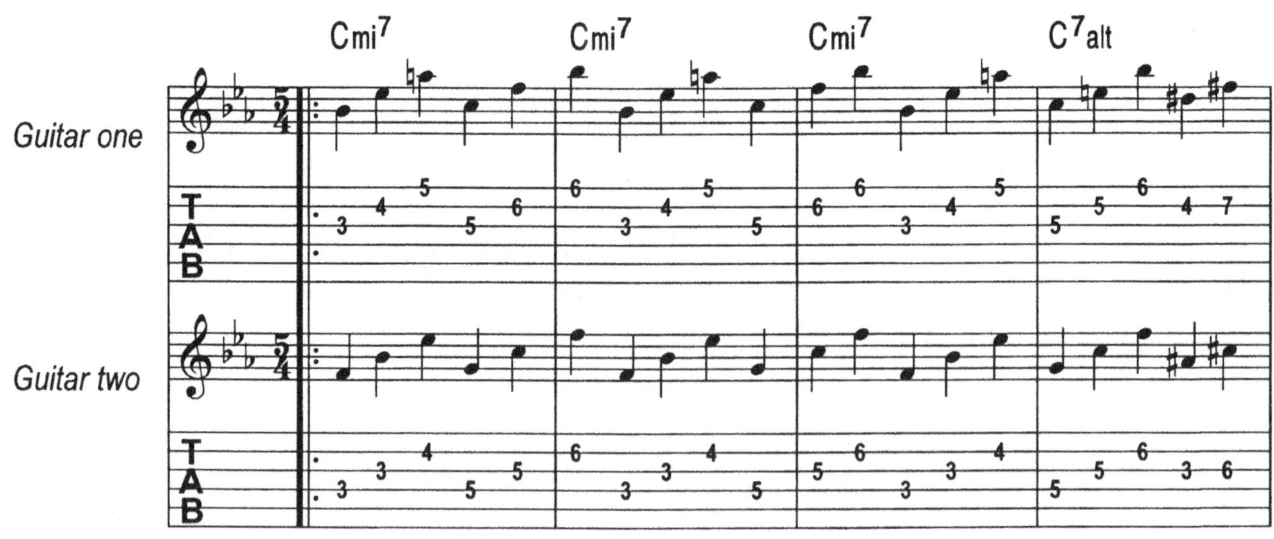

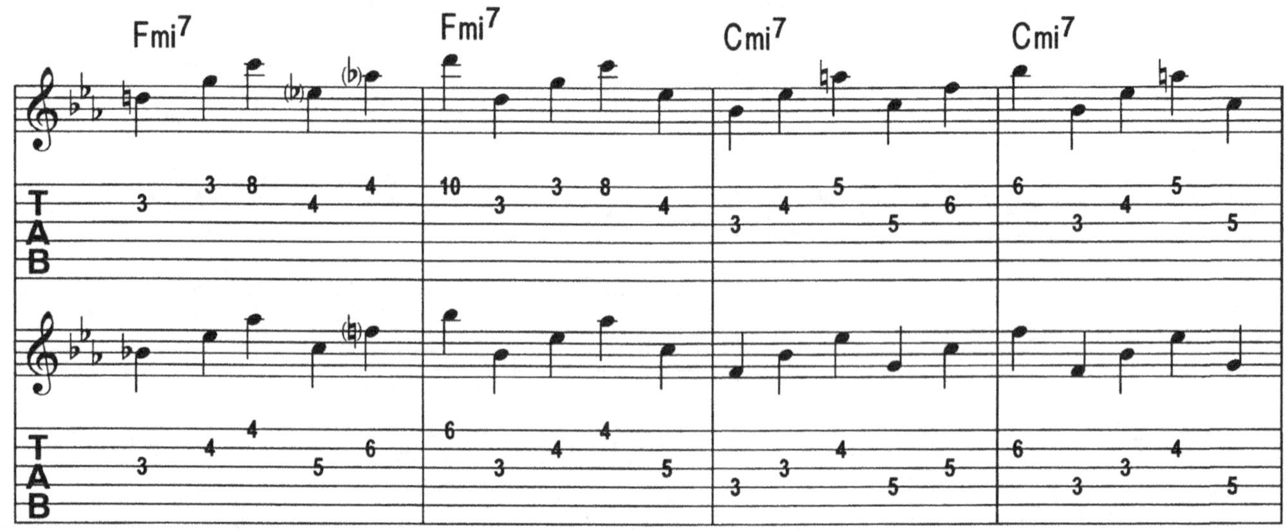

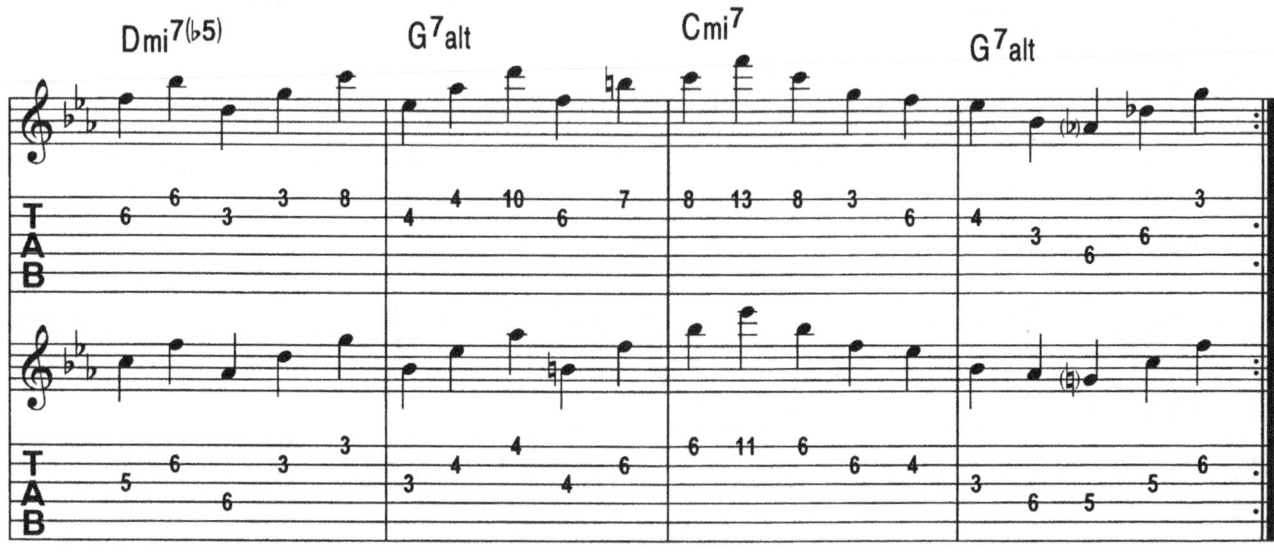

chapter four: reharmonization

For the final chapter, I'd like to explore just a few possibilities for reharmonization. Version **B** is similar to what is often considered a Charlie Parker style blues progression. You can see that Parker and other bebop musicians have added a series of secondary dominant progressions to the blues. The underlying harmonic movement (chords within the staff) is still the basic 12-bar blues with which we started. All of the techniques we have used thus far (among others) are viable here: harmonic & melodic minor, pentatonic scales and fourth voicings.

B

ii-V7 key of D minor

iii-VI-ii-V in the key of the IV chord (in this case B♭)

Bar	1	2	3	4
Reharmonization	FMAJ7	Emi7(♭5) A7(♭9/#5)	Dmi7 G7	Cmi7 F7(♭9)
Staff	F7	F7	F7	F7

A series of ii-V s moving down in 1/2 steps going to Gmi7 (the ii chord) from the minor iv chord. A tritone substitution kind of sound.

Bar	5	6	7	8
Reharmonization		B♭mi7 E♭7	Ami7 D7	A♭mi7 D♭7
Staff	B♭7	B♭7	F7	F7

Bar	9	10	11	12
Reharmonization	Gmi7	C7(♭9)	D7(♭9)	Gmi7 C7
Staff	C7	B♭7	F7	C7

Charlie Parker, Dizzy Gillespie, Clifford Brown, Bud Powell and the many other wonderful musicians who invented bebop still sound fresh and valid today, some fifty-or-so years later. As guitarists we are faced with technical obstacles that must be overcome in order to sound convincing playing over chord changes such as the ones you see in the example above. Part of surmounting these obstacles is moving out of visual shapes and grids into a concept based more on sound (or the absence of sound).

The aim of the next study is to use the Parker blues changes with a melody that focuses on the upper structure of the chords and is inspired by George Garzone and his solo on "Have You Met Miss Jones" (George Garzone *Fours and Two's,* NYC Records #6024).

Study No. 8

Parker Blues emphasizing upper structure # 34 - also use practice tracks 48 & 49

Study No. 8 continued

John Coltrane used a specific chord progression that he superimposed over the chord changes on many standard jazz songs such as "Tune Up," "How High the Moon," "But Not For Me," "Confirmation" and others.

Original	Dmi7	G7	CMAJ7	CMAJ7
Coltrane	Dmi7 E♭7	A♭MAJ7 B7	EMAJ7 G7	CMAJ7

In Ex. 30 below there are just two examples of what can be done with these changes and a 12-bar major blues. The Coltrane changes are above the staff and the original changes are within the staff.

Ex. 27 Coltrane changes over F blues **also use practice tracks 50 & 51**

One question students often ask concerns superimposing chords such as these over a rhythm section playing the original changes is "Won't it sound wrong if I play the Coltrane changes while everyone else is playing the original changes?" The first step is to learn how to play on the Coltrane changes *then* try the superimposition. If the student really studies a Coltrane solo such as "Countdown" (**John Coltrane** ***Giant Steps*** **Atlantic 1311-2 rec. 1959**) my point will become clearer.

One other method of reharmonization is based on the cycle of 4ths or can be considered a series of secondary dominants. In Ex. 28 below I have taken this concept to an impractical degree. These reharmonization ideas work best when used in moderation.

Ex. 28

Cycles over F blues

In Study no. 9 below, I've superimposed the Coltrane changes on a B♭ blues. The rhythm section will play similar changes on the practice tracks but you can also try superimposing them on a standard jazz B♭ blues.

Blues or Not

Bruce Saunders

Study No. 9 B♭ blues emphasizing Coltrane changes # 35 - also use practice tracks 52 & 53

appendix a: practice tracks

Practice Tracks 36 & 37 # 36 & 37

F blues slow & fast

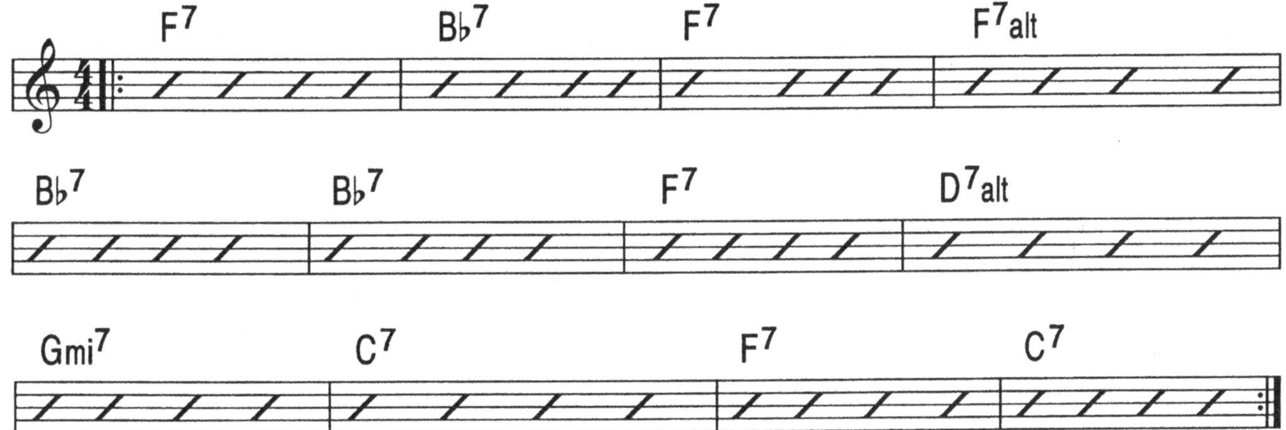

Practice Tracks 38 & 39 # 38 & 39

B♭ blues slow and fast

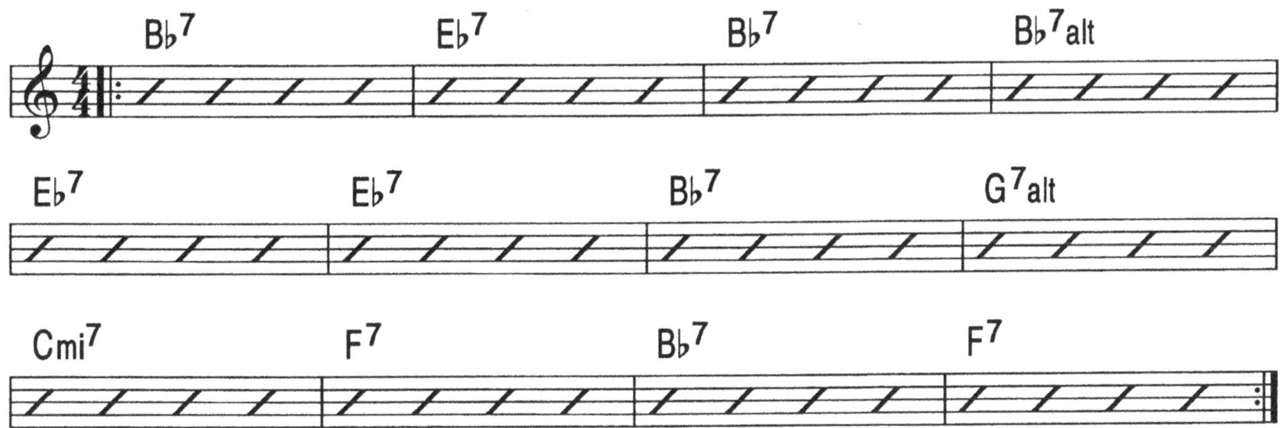

Practice Tracks 40 & 41 # 40 & 41

G blues slow and fast

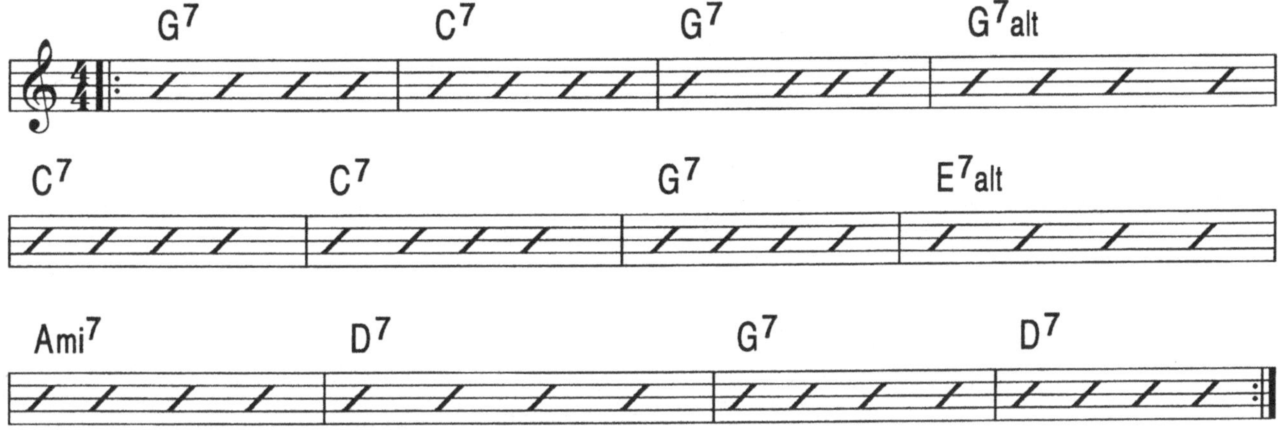

Practice Tracks 42 & 43 # 42 & 43

D♭ blues slow & fast

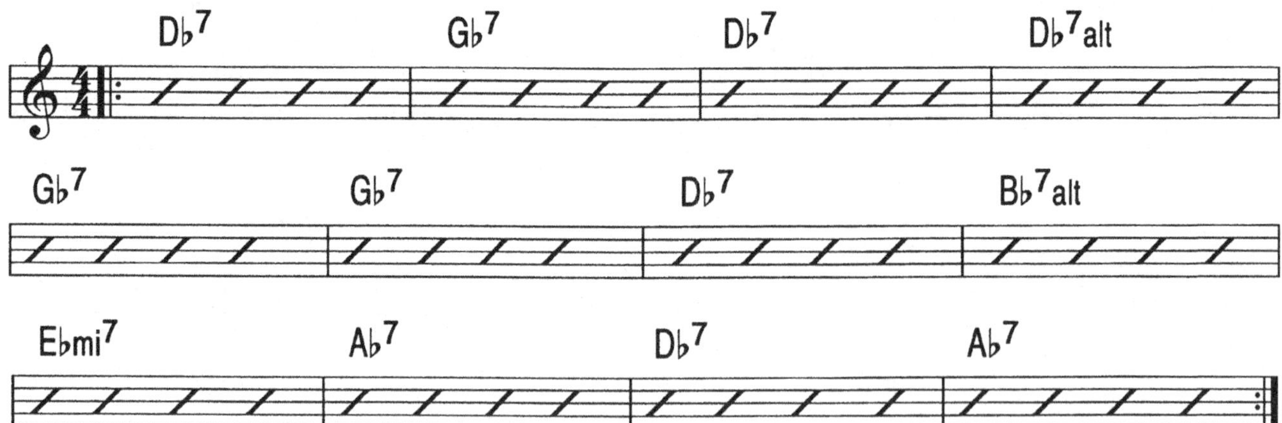

Practice Tracks 44 & 45 # 44 & 45

C minor blues slow & fast

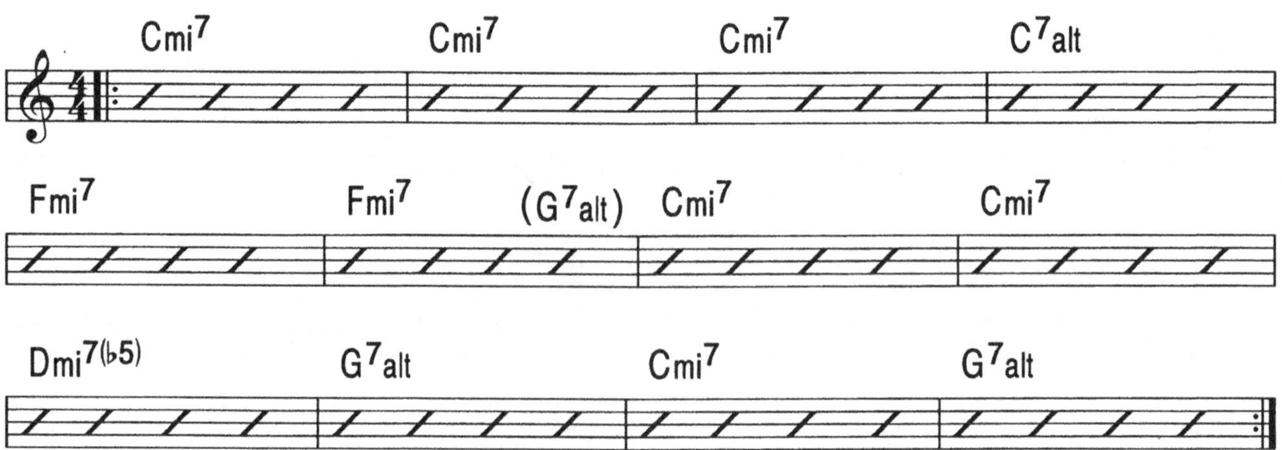

Practice Tracks 46 & 47 # 46 & 47

C minor 5/4 blues slow & fast

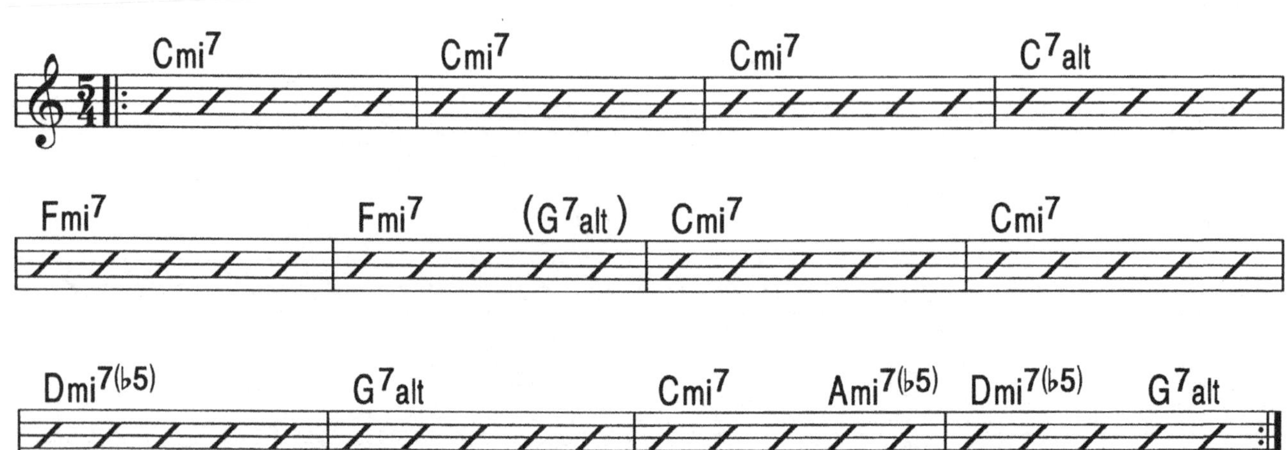

Practice Tracks 48 & 49 # 48 & 49

F Parker blues slow and fast

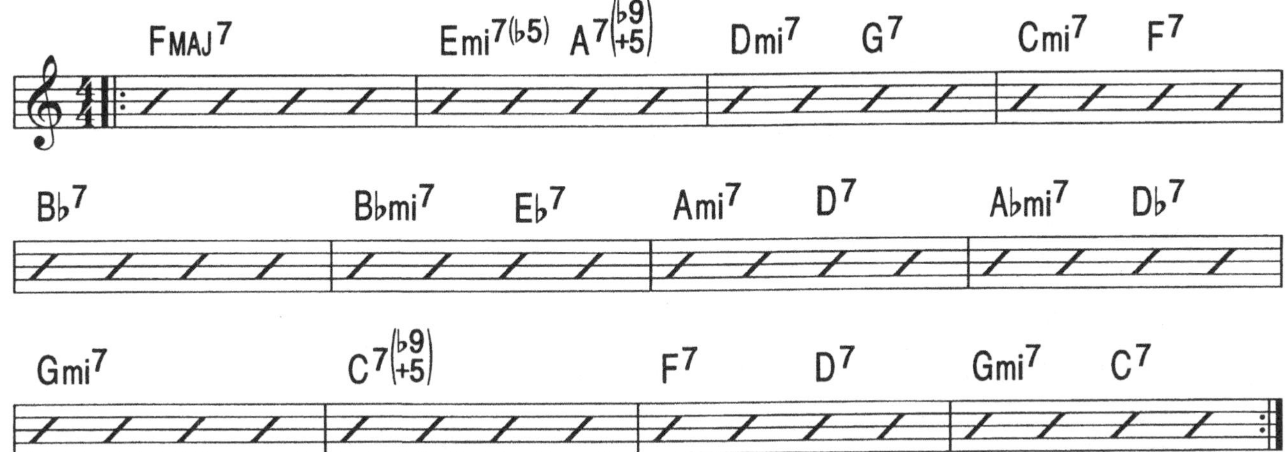

Practice Tracks 50 & 51 # 50 & 51

F Coltrane blues slow and fast

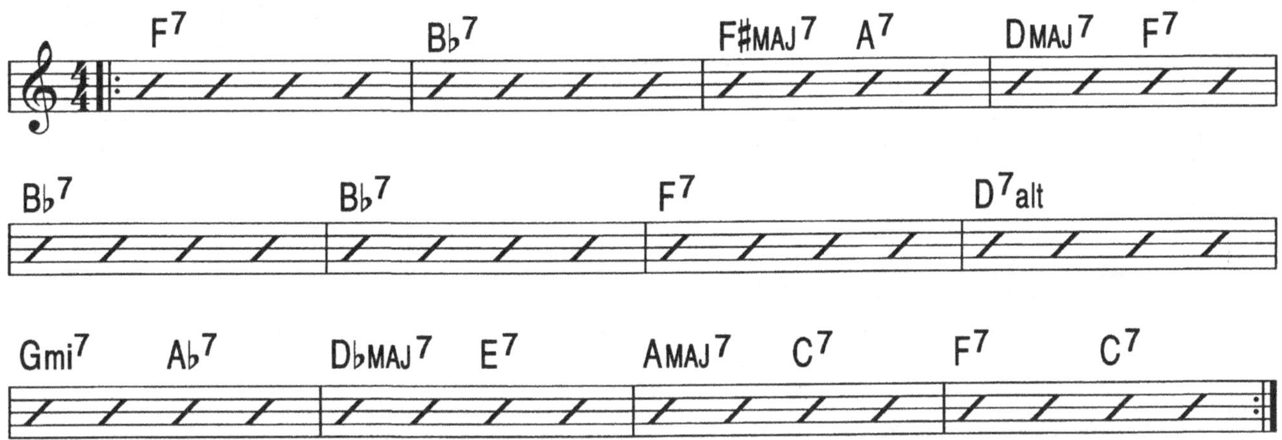

Practice Tracks 52 & 53 # 52 & 53

B♭ Coltrane blues slow and fast

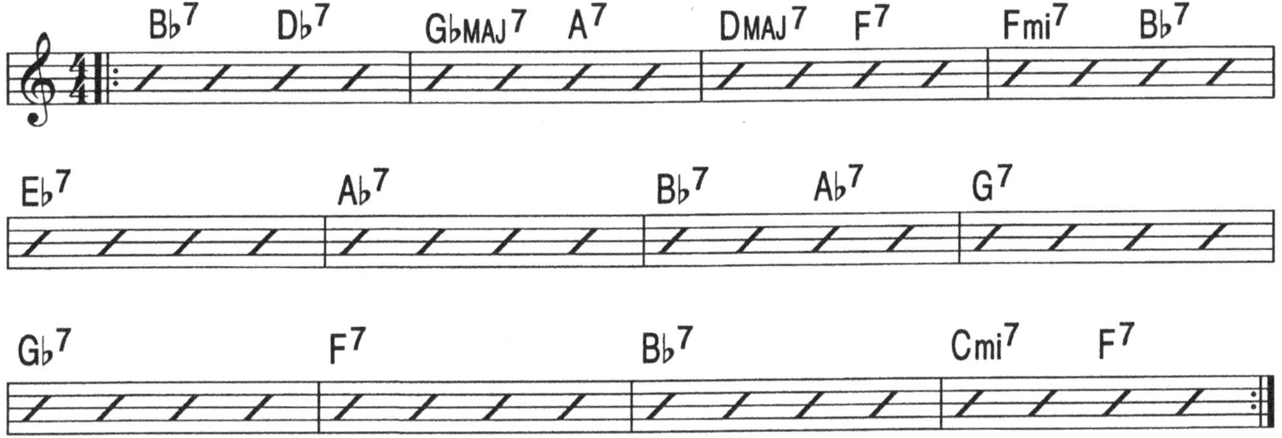

appendix b: alternate pentatonic vertical elements

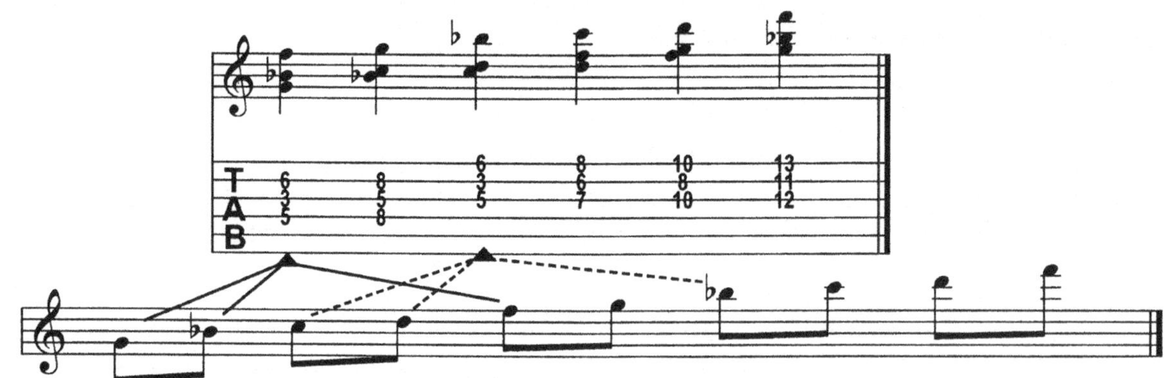

Ex. 29 # 54

Gmi7 pentatonic voicings (for use with Cmi7 or Gmi7 chords)

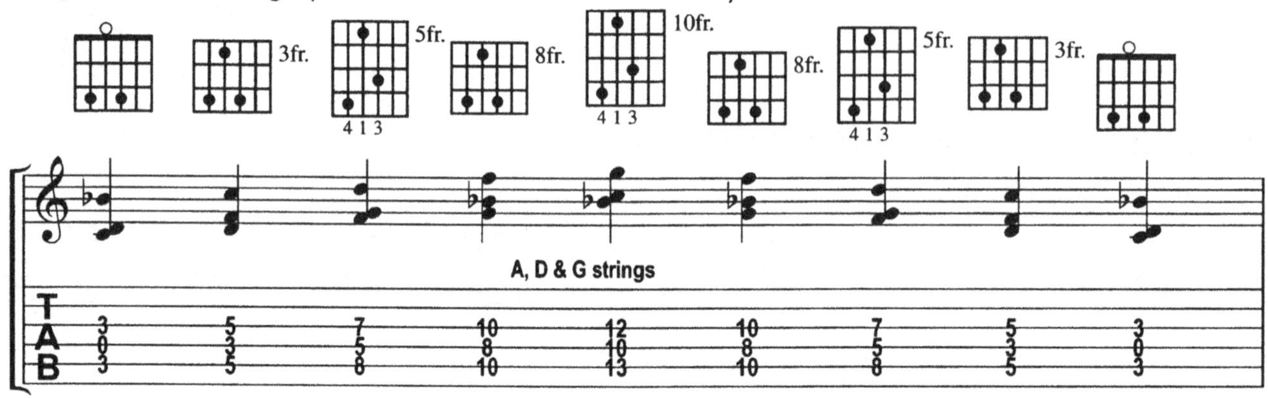

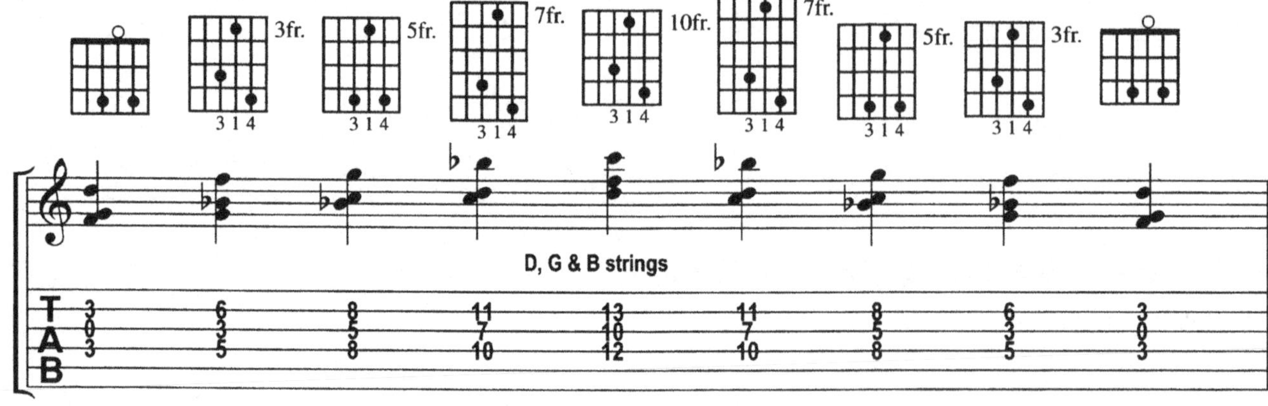

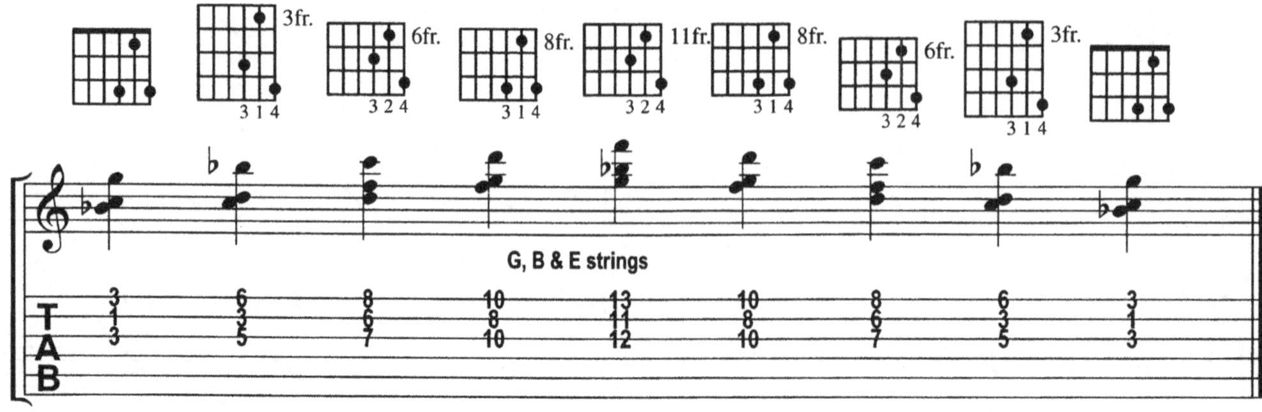

Ex. 30 💿 ***# 55***

Cmi7 pentatonic voicings (for use with Fmi7 or Cmi7 chords)

Ex. 31 # 56

Gmi7 pentatonic scale **fourth** voicings (use with Cmi7 or Gmi7chord)

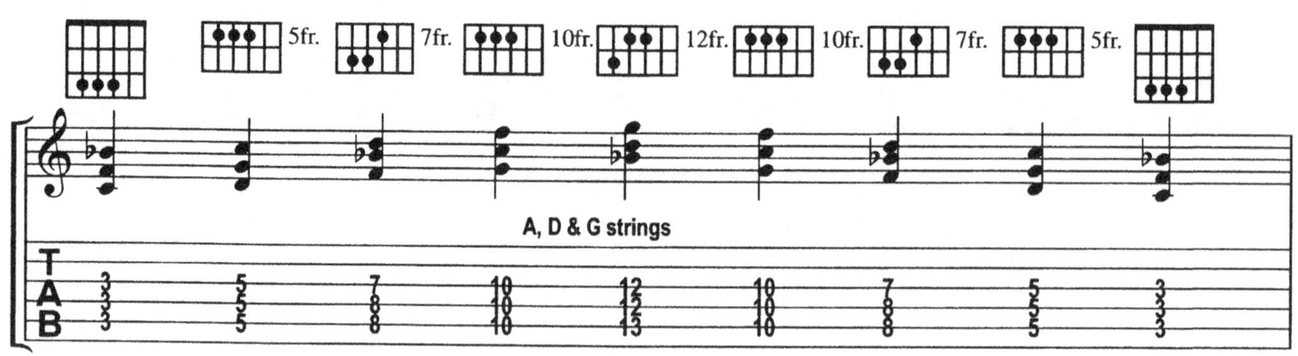

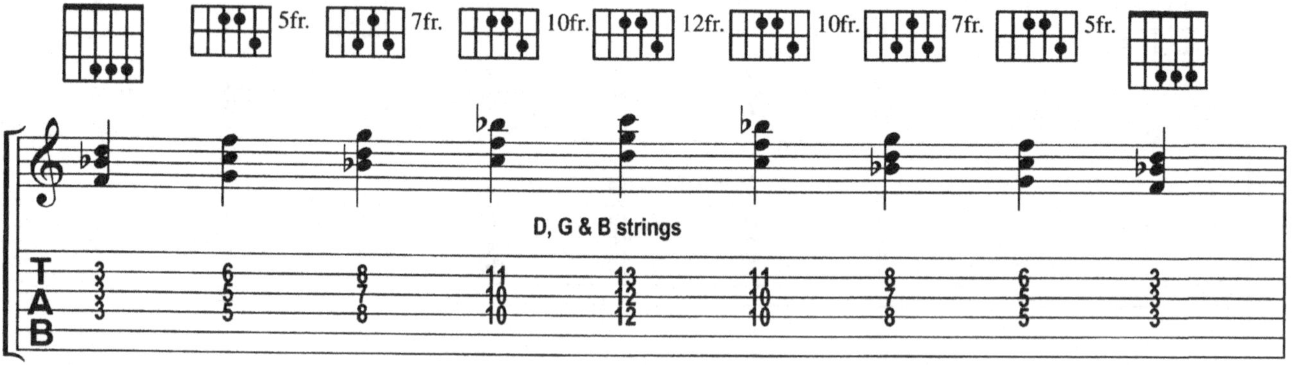

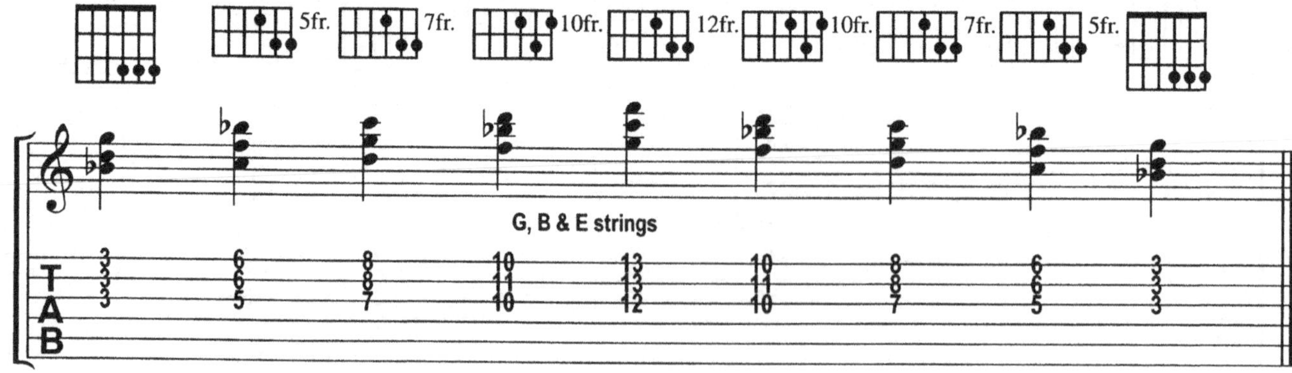

Ex. 32 # 57

Cmi7 pentatonic scale **fourth** voicings (use with Fmi7 or Cmi7 chord)

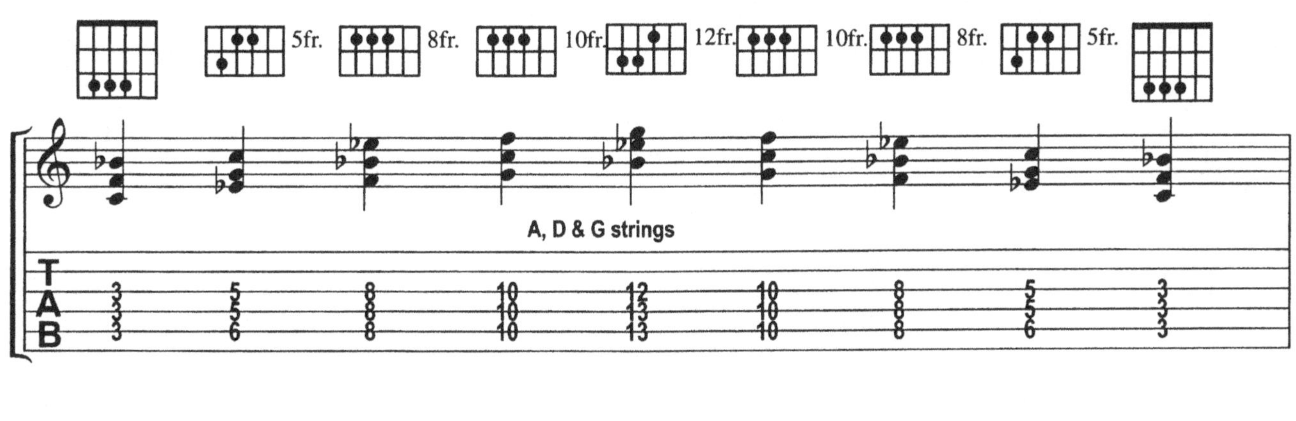

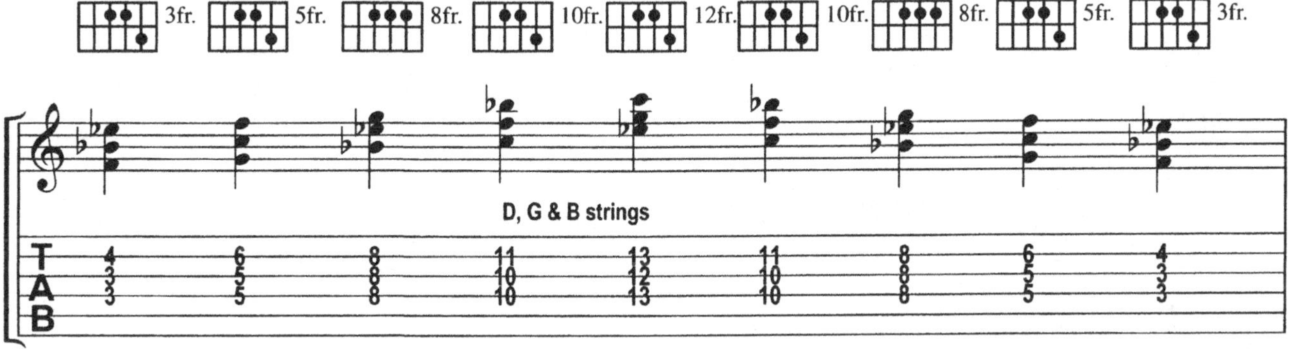

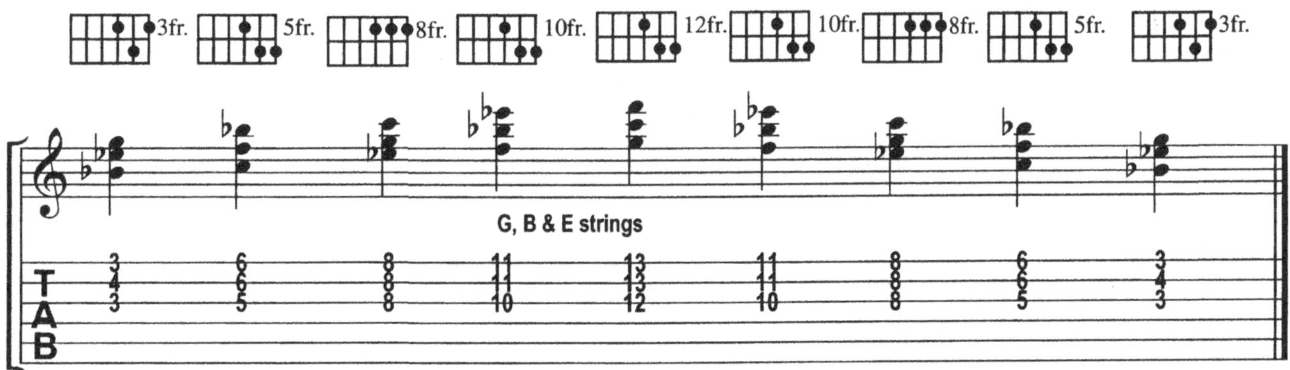

Alternate harmonic minor vertical elements

Ex. 33 # 58

C harmonic minor three-note **fourth** voicings (use with G7♭9♭13)

Ex. 34 # 59

F harmonic minor three-note **fourth** voicings (use with C7♭9♭13)

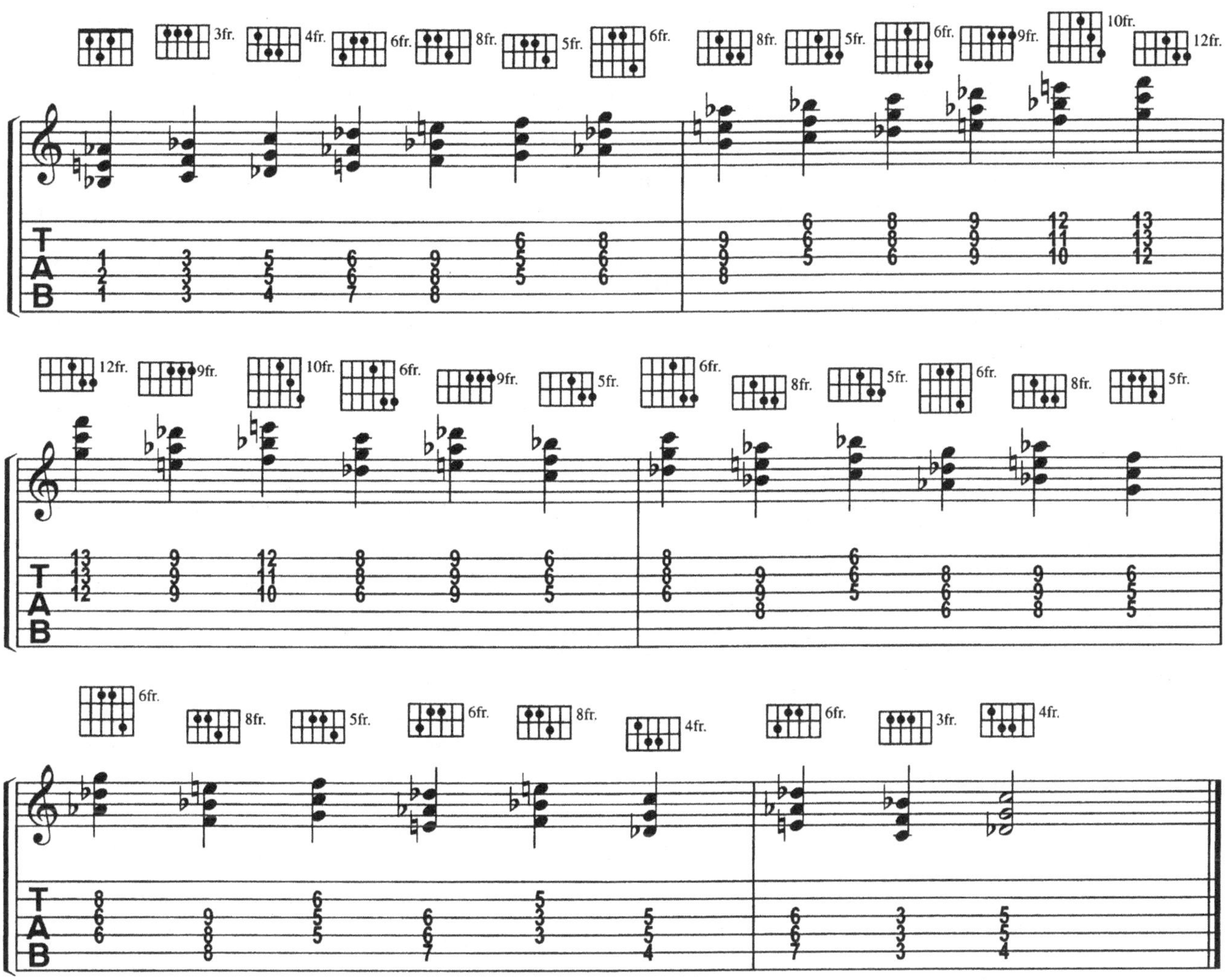

Ex. 35 # 60

C harmonic minor three-note (not fourths) voicings (use with G7♭9♭13)

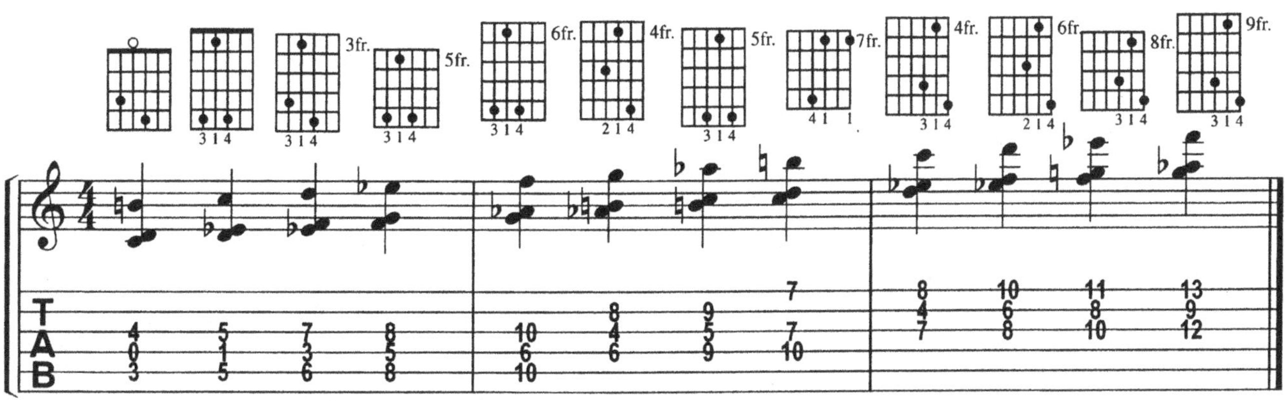

BRUCE SAUNDERS

Bruce Saunders is an award-winning guitarist, composer, author and educator. After receiving his Masters degree in jazz/classical guitar from the University of North Texas in 1986 he moved to New York city and began his musical career in earnest and has since recorded, performed and toured with some of the worlds best jazz musicians. A partial list would include: Jack DeJohnette, Dave Holland, Bill Stewart, Peter Erskine, Kenny Werner, Mark Murphy and many others. He performs regularly at many renowned New York jazz venues including Birdland, The Blue Note, Smalls, Fat Cat, The Jazz Standard, The Knitting Factory, Barbes, Detour, Smoke, Tonic and many others.

He has been a faculty member of the Berklee College of Music, one of jazz music education's most prestigious schools, since 1992. He has also taught at New York University, The New School and conducted many clinics and concerts in countries such as Colombia, Portugal, Mexico and Japan as well as throughout the United States.

He has four CDs as a leader and has played on approximately 35 other recordings. His newest recording is entitled 8 x 5 and was released on Mel Bay Records label in August of 2006. He is the author of four guitar method books published by Mel Bay.

Made in United States
Orlando, FL
25 February 2022

15139317R00030